Red Line 6

Workbook

Ausgabe für Bayern (Realschulen) Klasse 10

Herausgeber: Dr. Frank Haß

Ernst Klett Verlag
Stuttgart · Leipzig · Dortmund

English around the world

8/1 **1 Which of these fun facts about English do you think are true? Tick the sentences that you think are correct.**

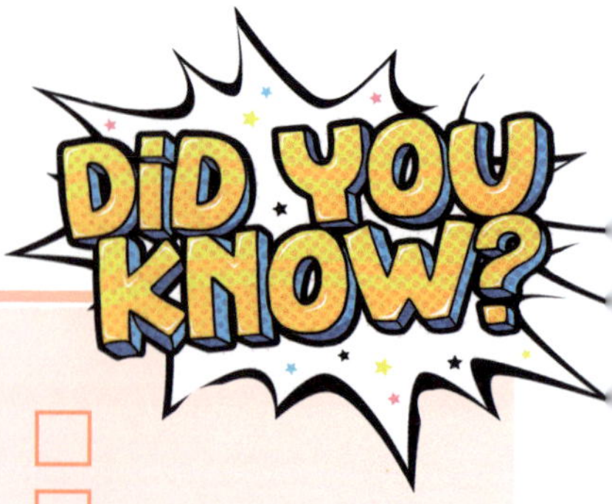

You can find the answers in the middle of your workbook on page 12.
Hint: Only four of the facts are false.

1. 'Town' is the oldest English word still used. ☐
2. About 80 % of everything on computers is in English. ☐
3. The word 'lol' cannot be found in a dictionary. ☐
4. The disease *Pneumonoultramicroscopicsilicovolcanoconiosis* is the longest English word. ☐
5. The letter A makes up 11 % of the English language. ☐
6. Great Britain means 'great land of the tattooed.' ☐
7. 'Bad' is the most common adjective in English. ☐
8. Some languages seem 'happier' than others; English is considered a happy language. ☐
9. English grammar is more difficult than most other languages. ☐
10. About twelve new words are added to the English language every day. ☐

1 9/3 **2 You will hear six students who are visiting an international English high school class in Germany. What reasons do the students have for joining the class?**

Write the correct numbers (1–5) in the boxes next to the words (A–H).
Be careful: Use each number only once.

A improve my English ☐
B live with a host family ☐
C speak German ☐
D eat different foods ☐
E stay with members of the family ☐
F find new friends ☐
G get to know another culture ☐
H live in a foreign country ☐

9/6 ↗ **3** **How important is English to you? Do this quiz and find out.**

Tick the answer that best describes you. Then add up how many times you picked a, b or c. Don't worry: There are no wrong answers.

1. Some tourists stop you in the street and ask for directions in English. You …
   a) give them detailed directions and make some additional suggestions of places they might like to see. ☐
   b) give them directions and politely wish them a nice day. ☐
   c) say sorry and run away as quickly as possible. ☐

2. You like to listen to music, but …
   a) only if it's in English. ☐
   b) you don't mind what language it is in. ☐
   c) you don't really like English songs. ☐

3. Who doesn't like a good film? But what about you?
   a) You prefer English films. ☐
   b) You watch English films only with subtitles. ☐
   c) It has to be in German and you hate subtitles. ☐

4. You go for an interview for a summer job and are told it will be in English.
   a) You can't wait to get started! ☐
   b) You are nervous but not worried. ☐
   c) You decide you don't need a job. ☐

5. Your school is starting an international class where all the subjects are taught in English. You …
   a) really hope you get chosen to join the class. ☐
   b) think it sounds interesting but won't be upset if you don't get chosen. ☐
   c) hope your English teacher forgets that you exist. ☐

6. English at school is …
   a) your favourite subject. ☐
   b) okay but not really that interesting. ☐
   c) is the subject you daydream a lot in. ☐

7. Your parents really want you to spend a year at an American high school. You …
   a) are already packing your suitcases. ☐
   b) say you will think about it. ☐
   c) start telling them how homesick you feel just thinking about it. ☐

8. When you go on vacation with your family and English is spoken, you …
   a) want to do all the talking. ☐
   b) usually let someone else talk. ☐
   c) you look for a bathroom quickly. ☐

A If you mostly picked a, you are a real English lover! Maybe you will end up living in the USA or Australia one day. If not, you will still probably find lots of places to practise your English.

B If you mostly picked b, you are probably better at English than you think, so don't be shy about talking to that American guy or girl! You may just make a new friend.

C If you mostly picked c, you need a bit of help with your English skills, but don't worry. Speaking English isn't just about grammar. A friendly smile and good listening skills can go a long way too!

The rainbow nation

separated | seat | final | Dutch | safari | diverse | gated
townships | natural | past | ethnic | unite | apartheid | reflect

11/3 **1 Complete the sentences about South Africa with the words in the boxes. There are more words than you need.**

1. South Africa is a very ethnically ________________ country with many people from different ____________ groups.
2. The president's __________ is in the main capital, Pretoria, where you can see influences from its colonial __________ .
3. If you want to see animals in their ___________ environment, then you have to go on a __________ .
4. South Africa had a very divided society, but the world cup ___________ helped somewhat to ___________ it.
5. The ___________ were the first European settlers in South Africa. Later, after independence from Europe, the government introduced the strict and unfair system of ______________________ .
6. South Africa is still a divided country, with many rich living in ___________ communites and the poor in _____________________ .

2 11/3 **2 Listen to the text about Sue's and David's trip to South Africa. Below is a list of six places, events and activities. Where did they do or see these things? Write the correct numbers in the boxes on the map.**

1. a ceremony
2. an exhibition
3. a boat trip
4. beaches
5. shopping
6. safari

13/4 ↗ **1** **Complete the following text. Use the correct forms of the verbs in the brackets and find words of your own to replace the question marks.**

A great view of Cape Town

Cape Town (1) ____________ (have) many great activities for teenagers of all ages! The first stop for most people is the spectacular coastline and the beautiful beaches. Of course, the beaches (2) _______ (be) fun to relax on, (3) ____________ (???) if you want to be more active, why not try a surfing lesson or go (4) ________________________ (swim)? You could even catch a glimpse of some seals or whales in the water with you. Wildlife lovers might also like to volunteer (5) ____________ (???) a day at a penguin rescue centre where you can clean and feed rescued penguins.

For a different perspective of life in Cape Town, you could take a township cycling tour where you can (6) ______________ (learn) about the traditional culture of the city. And, of course, no trip to Cape Town is complete without a hike up Table Mountain (7) __________ (???) enjoy the breathtaking view! After all that exercise, you will probably (8) ________ (be) hungry! The Canal Walk (9) _________________ (open) in 2000 and is now one of the most popular shopping centres for the wealthier residents of Cape Town. You can try many different cuisines at its restaurants and cafés. There is also a cinema and many shops (10) _______________ (???) clothes and souvenirs are available to buy.

14/6 ↗ **2** **Write the missing verbs in the sentences. Use the plural forms of the verbs. Be careful: Sometimes different tenses are possible.**

1. The army *are leaving* ______________ (to leave) the country now because the war is over.
2. The committee ____ (to start) a new project for teenagers next month.
3. Right now the company __________________________ (to fight) to stay in business.
4. The gang ______________________________ (to argue) with the shop owner when the police arrived.
5. The enemy ____________________ (to be) very near our border last night.
6. The group _______________________________________ (to ride) their bikes since six o'clock this morning.
7. My family ____ (to look forward to) going to South Africa since 2020.
8. The crew on the ship ____________________ (to be) very busy during the storm yesterday.

3 14/6 **3** You will hear an interview with an expert on gangs in Cape Town. Tick the correct sentence ending.

1. Jabu works for …
   a) the police. ☐
   b) a youth charity. ☐
   c) a school. ☐
   d) a gang. ☐

2. He says that many people who join gangs …
   a) are poor. ☐
   b) take drugs. ☐
   c) aren't from Cape Town. ☐
   d) join with friends. ☐

3. In South Africa almost half of young people …
   a) are in gangs. ☐
   b) have lost their job. ☐
   c) are from poor homes. ☐
   d) aren't in school. ☐

4. He thinks they …
   a) need new jobs. ☐
   b) need better towns. ☐
   c) need to learn skills. ☐
   d) need to stay safe. ☐

5. A positive gang is …
   a) rich. ☐
   b) similar to a family. ☐
   c) in a home. ☐
   d) in a school. ☐

6. He says young people could …
   a) make more money. ☐
   b) stop gangs. ☐
   c) repair townships. ☐
   d) work in prisons. ☐

Before you listen read all the questions. Look for key words. Then listen for these key words while you are listening. For example, the words 'positive' and 'gang' in question 5 are key words. Take notes of useful facts.

14/7 **4** Use a relative pronoun to make one sentence out of two.

1. We went to a restaurant in Cape Town. It attracts a lot of teenagers.
   We went to a restaurant in Cape Town which/that attracts a lot of teenagers.
2. I talked to my cousin. He goes to South Africa a lot for work.
   ____
3. She went to a big market. You could find delicious food there.
   ____
4. We had a great tour guide. His jokes were really funny.
   ____
5. I read about some gang members. They helped to repair houses in the townships.
   ____
6. We saw a band. It played amazing African music.
   ____
7. Here is the address of the hotel. We liked it the best.
   ____

15/10 **5** (MEDIATION) **Beantworte die Fragen stichpunktartig auf Deutsch.**

English in South Africa

Most people in South Africa speak more than one language. English is understood nearly everywhere. However, you may hear some words you don't understand because some words from other languages are used too.

Most children's first language is an African language, so many African words have found their way into the English language. People often say 'eish' at the beginning of a sentence to sound surprised. This word comes from the Xhosa language. Many words have also been taken from Zulu, such as 'bonsella' for a 'present' or a 'bonus', 'gogo' for 'grandmother' and 'muti' to mean traditional African medicine.

Many words have been taken from Afrikaans, a language which comes from several Dutch dialects. Almost everywhere you will hear people say 'ja' for 'yes'. If you are invited to a 'braai' (barbecue) you might describe the food as 'lekker' (nice or good) or maybe even 'vrot' (no good)! If someone calls you 'dof' (stupid) you might be angry, but if someone calls you 'kwaai' (cool) you should be happy.

Some English words have another meaning in South Africa. For example, 'robot' means 'traffic light' and a 'café' is also a 'corner shop'. A phrase that seems strange to visitors is 'just now' because it means 'later' and not 'now'. Even when South Africans say 'now now' it still doesn't mean 'now' but 'just as soon as they can'.

A Zulu show in Cape Town

1. Welche Sprache musst du beherrschen, um dich mit den meisten Südafrikanern verständigen zu können?

2. Warum kann es eventuell trotzdem vorkommen, dass man manche Wörter nicht versteht?

3. Warum gibt es im südafrikanischen Englisch so viele afrikanische Wörter?

4. Nenne zwei afrikanische Sprachen.

5. Woher kommt Afrikaans?

6. Warum kann es zu Missverständnissen kommen, wenn Besucher das dort gesprochene Englisch hören?

18/6 1 Read the text *Howzit, South Africa?* in your book on pages 16–17 again.

a) Are the sentences 1–10 'True' (T) or 'False' (F)? Choose 'Not in the text' (N) if there is not enough information to answer 'True' or 'False'. Tick (✓) the correct answer.

	T	F	N
1. Katlego will have his own room soon.	☐	☐	☐
2. Katlego has the same hobby as his brother.	☐	☐	☐
3. Katlego watches Trevor Noah's American TV show.	☐	☐	☐
4. Katlego's mum thinks he should be more realistic.	☐	☐	☐
5. Ruby used to live with her aunt and her cousin.	☐	☐	☐
6. Ruby is going to start a job with an AIDS charity when she leaves school.	☐	☐	☐
7. Ruby's aunt's death had a big impact on her.	☐	☐	☐
8. Alexa speaks three languages.	☐	☐	☐
9. Alexa has friends from different cultures.	☐	☐	☐
10. Alexa wants to study Business Studies at university.	☐	☐	☐

b) Now think of two more sentences and ask your partner to tick the correct answer.

	T	F	N
1. ______________________	☐	☐	☐
2. ______________________	☐	☐	☐

18/6 2 (WRITING) A big dream

Lots of people have dreams, especially when they are young. What do you think Tom's big dream has been since he was a child? Look at the photo story and write a short text about Tom and his dream. What did he do as a child or teenager? Did his parents support him? What was the most challenging experience? How did his dream come true? Write about 200 words in your exercise book.

20/4 ## 1 Complete the puzzle.

1. … it will be sunny tomorrow!
2. 
3. This is a short phrase often used in adverts.
4. He or she is the head of a sports team.
5. The crowd … when they won the World Cup!
6. Jacob Zuma is a … president of South Africa.
7. This is an area in a city or a town.
8. Different African … are spoken in South Africa.
9. This is a person who works in politics.
10. This is a very popular game in South Africa.

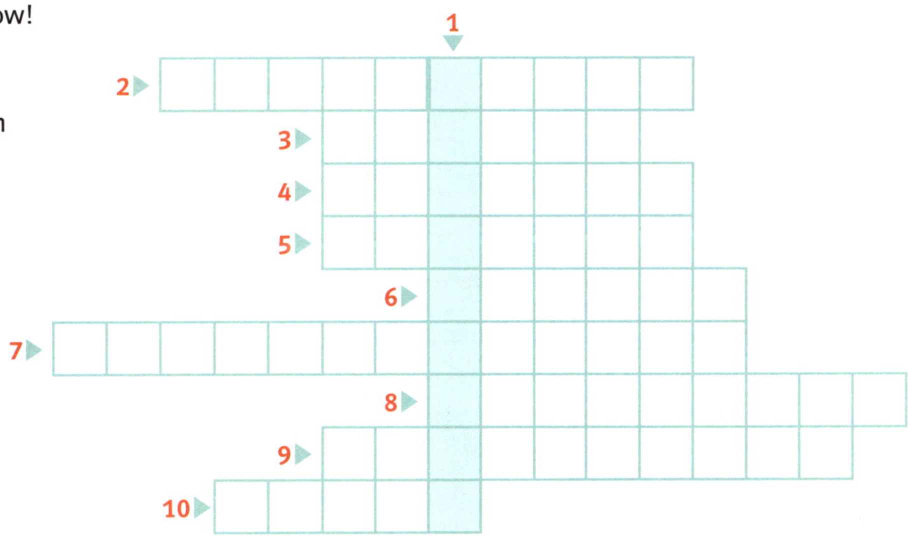

21/5 ## 2 Look at the timeline of events in South Africa. Write sentences in the simple past or present perfect.

since 1996:	South Africa has new constitution
2003:	government starts new programme to treat AIDS
2009–2018:	Jacob Zuma is president
2010:	World Cup in South Africa
2013:	Nelson Mandela dies
since 2020	more schools become digital because of COVID-19

1. ______________________________
2. ______________________________
3. ______________________________
4. ______________________________
5. ______________________________
6. ______________________________

4 21/6 **3 Listen to an expert talking on the radio about challenges in South Africa.**

a) Listen and take notes. You do not have to write complete sentences, but one word is not enough.

1. South Africa is famous for:
   - beautiful beaches
   - ____________________
   - ____________________
2. Problems:
   - high unemployment
   - ____________________
   - ____________________
   - ____________________
3. Solutions:
   - ____________________
   - ____________________
   - ____________________
4. Many black people:
   - ____________________
   - ____________________

b) What are the biggest challenges in your country? What do you think are the solutions to these problems? Write down three ideas and then talk to your partner.

____

____

____

____

____

21/7 ↗ **4** **Write about Thabo's life in a township in South Africa.**

Thabo is 14 years old and lives in a township in Johannesburg. Write sentences using the simple past and the past perfect once in each sentence. Don't forget to also add the correct articles and prepositions when needed.

1. before Thabo go to the spaza shop (a small store) • he ask mother what she needed
   Before Thabo went to the spaza shop, he had asked his mother what she needed.
2. Thabo fetch water from outside • before mother wash their clothes
3. when he find friends after school • they already start football game
4. after Thabo have haircut barber shop • go church
5. his father help neighbours fix their home • because they help him last year
6. before Thabo start school • he receive school uniform
7. children in the township not go to school • before apartheid end

22/9 ↗ **5** **(SPEAKING) Compare the two photos. Think of at least three differences.**

Use the information that you have learned about South Africa in this unit to support your ideas. Then talk to your partner and compare the differences you both found.

A Soweto township in Johannesburg

A gated community in Johannesburg

26/6

1 Read these tips before you read the text in exercise 2.

In your final exam, you may get a text which is mixed up. You will be asked to put the paragraphs in the correct order. Here are some tips that will help you do that:

- *Look for a sentence that introduces the subject of the text. This is probably the first parapraph.*
- *Look at the last sentence of the first paragraph. What is it about? Can you find another paragraph that goes into more detail about this?*
- *Read the paragraphs and continue to look closely at the last sentence of each paragraph. This will help you find the paragraph that comes next.*
- *Underlining the main ideas in the text will also help you to sort the paragraphs.*
- *The last paragraph should have some type of closing statement or list some very current facts.*
- *When you think you have the correct order, read the whole text through. Does the text make sense?*
- *Don't panic if you don't find the correct order right away. The more you look at the text, the clearer the order will become.*

26/6

2 Brenda Fassie – Queen of African Pop

The following text is about Brenda Fassie, a famous South African singer. The paragraphs of the text are mixed up. Put the different parts (A–G) into the correct order (1–7). Write your answers in the gird below. One part (B) has already been put in the correct place.

A Fassie suddenly had money and fame. She spent her money on houses, cars and big parties. She had a son called Bongani and married a businessman. However, the marriage ended in divorce after just a year. Fassie was disappointed and started taking drugs. Her career suffered and she sometimes didn't go to her own concerts. Her money was all spent and she lost her house.

B More disappointment came when her song *Black President* (about Nelson Mandela and his recent release from prison) was banned by the apartheid government. Fassie recorded more songs, now with a more African sound. She stopped singing in English, saying she was "proud to be African", but still couldn't find a hit. When her girlfriend died, she finally got help with her drug addiction.

C Just three years later, South Africans were shocked at the news that she had been taken to hospital at the age of just 39. Her fans hoped and prayed that she would be OK, but after two weeks, the news came that she had died. The whole of South Africa was sad at losing their first black pop star.

D Fassie's father died when she was just two years old and the family's life became even harder. Her mother, who worked as a cleaner, recognized her daughter's extraordinary singing talent early, and by the time she was four, she was singing at church events while her mother played the piano. At the age of 16, she left her township and went to Soweto to become a singer.

E Brenda Fassie was a superstar of South African music. Although her life was difficult, her music was loved by all. When she was born in 1964, her parents named her after an American singer called Brenda Lee, a sign, perhaps, of her future talent. She was the youngest of nine children and the family lived in poverty in a township near Cape Town.

F Her first group was called Joy. After this she became the singer in a township pop group called Brenda and the Big Dudes. In 1983 their first song was released. It was called *Weekend Special* and was about a boyfriend who would only see Brenda at the weekend. It was a big hit and soon Fassie and her band were touring the world.

G After Fassie had stopped taking drugs, she found success with her album *Memeza*. It became the most popular South African album of 1998 and won many awards. She then released an album every year for the next few years and toured Africa and America. In 2001 she appeared in the American magazine *Time*, in an article called 'The Madonna of the Townships'.

1	2	3	4	5	6	7
				B		

26/6 **3** **List the tips from exercise 1 that were useful for you. Can you think of any other tips?**

____

____

____

____

____

26/6 **4** **Answer the questions about Brenda Fassie.**

1. What events made Fassie's life difficult? (Write at least three facts.) ______________________________
2. How did Fassie's life change after the success of *Weekend Special*? ______________________________
3. Why do you think *Black President* was banned? ______________________________
4. Was Fassie only popular in Africa? How do you know? ______________________________

Lösungen online
ae8fx7

___/6P 1 I can understand information about South Africa.

→p. 16/1

Hang out with the penguins

There aren't many places in the world where you can get close to penguins and even swim with them. But you can at Boulders Beach, just 45 minutes away from Cape Town. The penguin colony at Boulders Beach is one of only a few in the world, and it has become very famous and popular. You can sit on the beach with the penguins or swim with them. You might even have to share your beach towel with one of them, but you should not touch or feed them. You can also see whales, sharks or dolphins in the bay. Boulders Beach is part of the Table Mountain National Park, where you can go hiking, take a cable car trip to the top of the mountain or visit an old silver mine and learn about the past.

Answer the questions.

1. What type of text is this? a) an e-mail ☐ b) an ad ☐ c) a short article ☐
2. Where is Boulders Beach? ______
3. Why is the beach so popular and what can you do there? ______
4. What else can you see in the bay? ______
5. Where does the cable car go? ______
6. Where can you go if you are interested in history? ______

___/5P 2 I can give tips for travelling.

→p. 16/2

Write a short text about why your town would be fun for teenagers to visit. Write about 100 words.

______

___/8P 3 I can understand texts about the hopes and dreams of young people.

→ p. 17/3

Look at the article on pages 16–17 in your book again. Who is it? Katlego, Ruby or Alexa?

1. needs to find a job next year ______
2. thinks happiness is more important than success ______
3. is inspired by a comedian ______
4. wants to help society ______
5. often fights with parents about the future ______
6. wants to become a surfing coach ______
7. wishes black communities could educate people better ______
8. wants to have more space ______

___/4P 4 I can give my opinion about a political issue.

→ p. 17/4

Think about what you learned about apartheid in the unit. Write a political comment about it. Write about 50 words. You can use these phrases:

It was very unfair …

Blacks and whites were not treated equally …

It still affects how people live today.

______

______

______

______

______

___/8P 5 I can understand a text about a famous person.

→ p. 17/5

Look at the text on pages 12–13 again. Are the sentences true (T), false (F) or not in the text (N)? Tick the correct answer.

	T	F	N
1. Brenda Fassie had eight younger brothers and sisters.	☐	☐	☐
2. When Fassie was young, she loved to sing in church.	☐	☐	☐
3. *Weekend Special* was the name of Fassie's first group.	☐	☐	☐
4. Fassie liked to buy houses and cars.	☐	☐	☐
5. Not all of Fassie's songs were in English.	☐	☐	☐
6. Fassie liked the article *Time* magazine wrote about her.	☐	☐	☐
7. She died at the age of 39.	☐	☐	☐
8. There are now statues of Fassie in South Africa.	☐	☐	☐

Lösungen online
ae8fx7

○ 1 I can understand information about South Africa.

The rainbow nation

South Africa is the most southern country in Africa, and it shares borders with six other African countries.
Since apartheid ended, South Africa has been known as the 'rainbow nation' because South Africa has a multicultural society where people from different nations are able to live together peacefully. The people of South Africa still remember their difficult history, and there are a lot of social differences, but they are proud of their country. They love sports and celebrate their national teams, and they are also proud of their amazing wildlife. Many tourists come to take part in safaris in one of the many national parks or to enjoy the country's beautiful beaches.

Read the text and finish the sentences.

1. Six African states share ______________________________.
2. South Africa has been known ______________________________
   ______________________________.
3. South Africans are proud of their country despite its ______________________________.
4. Important tourist attractions include ______________________________.
5. Besides the wildlife, tourists can ______________________________
   ______________________________.

○ 2 I can give tips for travelling.

What can teenagers do if they visit your town? Complete the mind map with travel tips.

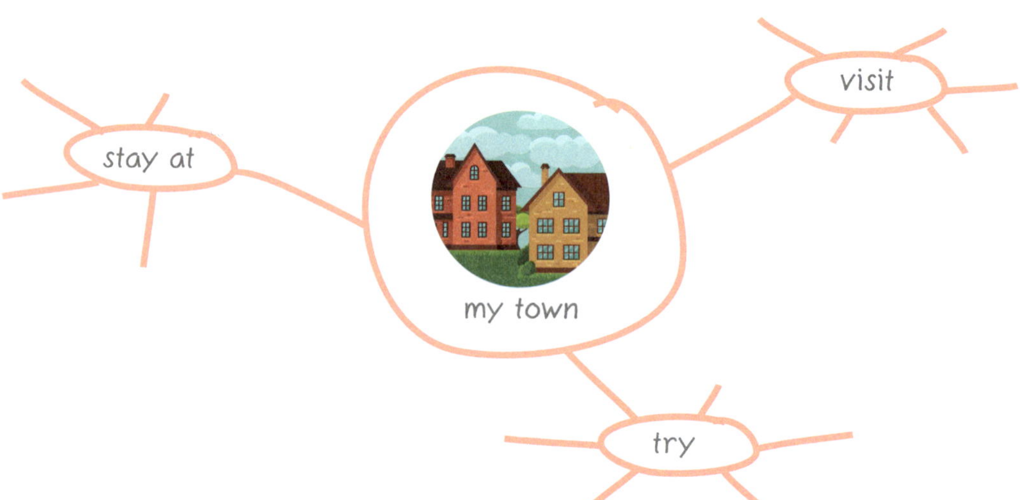

○ 3 I can understand texts about the hopes and dreams of young people.

Look at the article on pages 16–17 in your book again and answer the questions.

1. What does Katlego's mother call his dream? ______________________
2. Who is Katlego's role model? ______________________
3. How did Ruby's aunt die? ______________________
4. Who said Ruby should do volunteer work? ______________________
5. Where does Alexa live? ______________________
6. Which languages does Alexa speak? ______________________

○ 4 I can give my opinion about a political issue.

Many teenagers are worried about the future. For example, they do not think the government is doing enough to protect the environment. What do you think? Write your opinion. Write about 150 words in your exercise book. The ideas below can help you, but you don't have to use or agree with them.

- Examples for better laws to protect the environment.
- Make things like electric cars and solar panels cheaper.
- Work together with other countries.
- Encourage people to walk, cycle or use trains.
- Invest more in renewable energy.

○ 5 I can understand a text about a famous person.

Look at the text on pages 12–13 again. Are the sentences true (T) or false (F)? Tick the correct answer.

	T	F
1. Brenda Fassie was named after a famous British singer.	☐	☐
2. Fassie was a young child when she started singing for people.	☐	☐
3. Fassie joined more than one group during her career.	☐	☐
4. Fassie never missed any of her own concerts.	☐	☐
5. The apartheid government did not like her song about Nelson Mandela.	☐	☐
6. All of Fassie's songs were in English.	☐	☐
7. She was very successful after she had stopped taking drugs.	☐	☐
8. Fassie had been in hospital for three years before she died.	☐	☐

Here you can improve your skills by doing a reading exercise.

31/3 ## 1 Read this story about Amahle.

Apartheid was a way of life for me; it was all I had ever known. My dad, a teacher, was killed by a police officer during protest when I was a baby. I don't remember him. I just know that we didn't talk about politics, and we tried to stay out of trouble. But the police still came to our house in the night every few months, and we were forced from our beds, crying and confused.
Our house was in a black township. We had no electricity, no bathroom. My mum went to work every day, and my grandma and aunts helped to look after me and my brother and sister. We all had to leave school and work as soon as we were 13 because we needed the money for our family. Mum found it hard to look after three children. I dreamed of going to university and getting an office job, but as soon as I left school, I started working in the kitchen of a white family. I was angry at the world. I thought all my problems were caused by white people; they had taken my dad, they had killed my dreams, and they treated us like animals.

It was early February in 1990 when we heard an announcement on TV. They told us apartheid was going to end. We were so happy. We sang and laughed and cried all night. But in real life, nothing much changed quickly; it took a long time to really end apartheid.
I left my job in the kitchen and found work in a small restaurant in a nice part of the town. One day, when I looked out of the kitchen window, I saw an old, white man come in. He was tall with grey hair. I had seen his face on TV – he had been an important police officer in the apartheid system. He was the man who had told the police to attack the protesters when my father was killed. I was angry! How could he sit there, eating in a restaurant when he had been responsible for so many deaths? When his food was ready, I decided to take it to him myself. I put the plate in front of him, looked straight into his grey eyes and said, "You killed my father."
I didn't wait for an answer. I just returned to the kitchen.

When the restaurant closed nearly two hours later, I noticed he was still there, sitting alone in the corner. He looked at me. "Can I talk to you?" he asked. I sat down opposite him. I wanted to feel equal. He didn't speak for a moment. "I'm sorry," he said. We spoke for an hour. I told him about my mum, about my life. He told me how he had started to fight against police violence towards black people. As he spoke, I thought of Nelson Mandela's words, "I knew if I didn't leave my bitterness and hatred behind, I'd still be in prison." If Mandela could forgive, then I knew I had to try too.

He stood to leave, holding out his hand to me. I took it in mine and looked him in the eye again. "I forgive you," I told him. I felt relief. I don't know if my mum or dad would have done the same, but I knew it was what I needed to do so I could live without hatred.

31/3 ## 2 Is the information true, false or not in the text?

Information that is not correct is false. If you cannot find the answer in the text, then the information is not in the text.

	T	F	N
1. A police officer killed Amahle's dad.	☐	☐	☐
2. Amahle's family was treated badly by the police.	☐	☐	☐
3. Amahle went to university after school.	☐	☐	☐
4. Amahle's family celebrated when Apartheid ended.	☐	☐	☐
5. Amahle liked her job in the restaurant.	☐	☐	☐
6. The police officer was looking for Amahle.	☐	☐	☐
7. The police officer was proud of what he had done.	☐	☐	☐
8. Amahle told her mother later about the officer.	☐	☐	☐

31/3 ## 3 Write facts in the boxes about the people in the story.

Here, you need to scan the text for particular details. You can skip whole sections if the information you need is not there. Instead, look for the information you need.

AMAHLE

AMAHLE'S DAD

AMAHLE'S MUM

OLD MAN

AMAHLE'S BROTHER AND SISTER

Lösungen online
ae8fx7

A sports crazy nation

5 32/1

1 You will hear statements from five people at a sports camp in South Africa. What are they doing?

Write the correct numbers (1–5) in the boxes next to the categories (A–H).
Be careful: Use each number only once.

A climbing ☐
B table tennis ☐
C kayaking ☐
D swimming ☐
E mountain biking ☐
F cricket ☐
G rugby ☐
H cross country running ☐

32/1

2 Complete the second sentence so that it has a similar meaning to the first sentence, using the KEY WORD given in brackets.

Do not change the KEY WORD given. You must use between two and five words including the KEY WORD.

1. To go swimming, you need to wear a swimming cap. (IF)
   You must wear a swimming cap _If you want_ to go swimming.
2. Tomorrow's activity is cricket, but if it's raining we'll play table tennis. (INSTEAD)
   Instead of playing cricket, we'll play table tennis tomorrow if it's raining.
3. Many people say this is the best sports camp in South Africa! (SAID)
   This is said to be the best sports camp in South Africa!
4. If you don't wear the correct equipment, you can't go climbing. (UNLESS)
   You can't go climbing _unless you wear_ the correct equipment.
5. Please be careful with the kayaks because they are very expensive. (WORTH)
   The _kayaks are worth_ a lot of money, so please be careful with them.
6. Two people won a 'fair play' prize yesterday. (WERE)
   There were two winners of the 'fair play' award yesterday.
7. She ran her fastest during the race. (AS)
   She ran _as fast as possible_ during the race.
8. He loved sports when he left the camp. (BY)
   By the time he left the camp, he had learned to love sports.

33/4 ↗ **3 Complete the following text. Use the correct form of the words in brackets.**

Our sports camp (1) ~~hat~~ opened ____________ (open) in 1997 to offer sports holidays for schools and teenage groups. It (2) war built ____________ (build) near a national reserve to the east of Cape Town. Now it (3) ____________ (become) one of (4) ____________ (large) sports camps in South Africa and offers a wide range of facilities. (5) ____________ (visit) to the centre can use our swimming pools, sports pitches, sports halls or enjoy (6) ____________ (explore) the natural (7) ____________ (surround) by foot, bike or horse. Next year we (8) ____________ (offer) water adventures on the river too. All our (9) ____________ (friend) teachers are fully trained and we provide (10) ____________ (employ) to many local people. Our guests can choose to stay in our hostel or to camp in our safari tents and can enjoy fresh, local cuisine in our (11) ____________ (dine) area.

33/4 ↗ **4 (SPEAKING) Finish the dialogue about a sports camp.**

a) Cover your partner's part of the dialogue with a piece of paper, but don't cover the arrows (→). Then act out the dialogue with your partner.

Partner A: You work at the sports camp.	Partner B: You've just arrived at the camp.
1. Begrüße Partner B und sage, wie du heißt.	1. ____________
2. ____________	2. Begrüße Partner A und sage, wie du heißt. Sage, dass du eine Woche bleibst.
3. Bejahe. Sage, dass er/sie im Hostel C bleiben wird.	3. ____________
4. ____________	4. Frage, wo das ist.
5. Antworte, das letzte Gebäude rechts.	5. ____________
6. ____________	6. Sage okay. Frage, wann es Abendessen gibt. Du hast Hunger nach deiner Reise.
7. Antworte, dass es das Essen um sechs Uhr gibt und danach Fußball gespielt wird.	7. ____________

b) Continue the dialogue with your partner. Talk about activities at the camp. For ideas look at exercise 1 on page 20.

Living in a global village

35/3 **1 Describe the average global village citizen.**

a) Look at the information in your book again about the global village. What would an average person in this village be like? What would they have? What wouldn't they have? Finish the description below. These words can help you: young, rich, speak, read, job, money and car.

The average citizen could be a man or a woman. He or she is probably quite young.

____

____

____

____

____

b) Are you like the average global village citizen? Say why or why not.

____

____

____

c) Why do you think most people now live in a city. Write three reasons.

____

____

____

____

____

37/3 **1 Fill in the missing words. You don't need all the words in the boxes. Put in the right verb forms.**

as a result	ensure	features	quality	solutions	increase
continue	key factor	reduce	residents	species	harmful

When engineers or architects are looking for (1) ________________ to certain problems, they sometimes copy (2) ________________ which they find in the natural world. This is called bionics. This was the case with the Japanese bullet train, one of the fastest in the world. But there was a problem when the train travelled through a tunnel. Air built up in front of the train and (3) ________________ there was a loud "boom" when it came out. This was uncomfortable for passengers and local (4) ________________ and (5) ________________ for wildlife. An engineer had an idea for improvement by observing the kingfisher, a small (6) ________________ of bird which catches fish in rivers. The (7) ________________ in its success is the shape of its bill or mouth – very thin at the tip, wider nearer its head. This (8) ________________ that the bird can move in the water silently and very fast without making the water cloudy. The engineers modelled the "nose" of their bullet train on the kingfisher's bill. Then there was no noise when the train left a tunnel. Since there was less air resistance, it was able to travel faster too, without (9) ________________ the amount of energy necessary. This meant that costs could be (10) ________________.

6
37/3 **2 Listen to the text and fill in the fact card about velcro.**

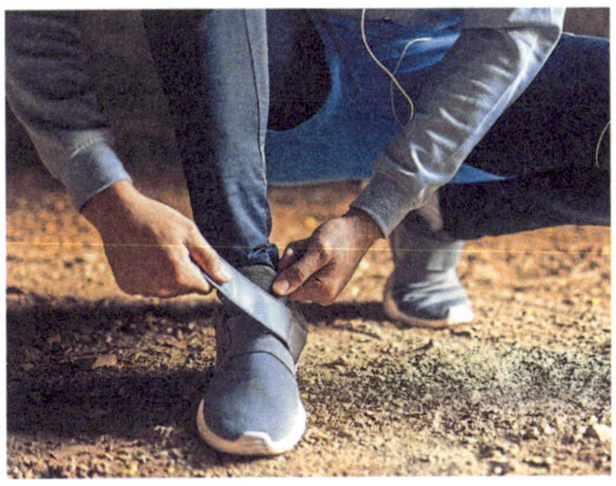

Place and time:

Switzerland in 1941

The inspiration for the invention:

____

How was the plant studied:

____

Description of the new product:

____

____

Two different uses:

____

38/6 ## 3 Say what these people are (not) planning for the future and why. Write six sentences below.

1. study medicine because need more specialists
2. not take driving test because not be any private cars
3. buy big field then grow own crops
4. move to Scandinavia because climate here be too hot
5. not become travel agent because everybody book vacations online
6. learn Mandarin because become global language

1. Hayley is going to study medicine because our society will ____________
2. I ____________
3. The Richmonds ____________
4. We ____________
5. Nathan ____________
____
6. Some of my friends ____________
____

38/7 ## 4 Complete the following text. Use the correct forms of the words in brackets and find words of your own to replace the question marks. There is one example.

The first Earth Day took (1) place ________ (???) in 1970 and now it (2) ________ (celebrate) every year in April. Activists are working (3) ________ (hard) to show the world how (4) ________ (dangerous) the situation is for our planet. If we do not protect our planet (5) ________ (good), the earth (6) ________ (suffer) even more from climate change. This (7) ________ (already cause) serious drought, floods and fires on several continents. On Earth Day 2016 the Paris Agreement (8) ________ (adopt) and 196 nations promised (9) ________ (???) limit global temperature rise to less (10) ________ (???) 2°C over pre-industrial levels. It is not certain (11) ________ (???) many countries (12) ________ (reach) this goal. At the moment there is a lack of activity and ambition in many countries. Some governments (13) ________ (not agree) to the agreement yet. But many people (14) ________ (not accept) this inaction. Almost every month there are protests and petitions either online (15) ________ (???) on the streets – and there are hopes that they (16) ________ (continue) in the future.

39/10

5 Look at the cartoons.

a) Match the captions to the cartoons. Write the correct number next to each caption. One of the cartoons does not have a caption.

☐ "Did you feel that bump?" "Oh please, I can't pay attention to everything!"

☐ "I don't mind you selling the car to be green but could we use the bus next time?"

☐ "Why do I need a driving license when I'm not even driving?!"

b) Which cartoon do you think is the best? Tell your group why.

c) One of the cartoons has no text. Can you think of a funny text for it?

43/8 1 **Read this excerpt from the book *Dry* by Neal Shusterman and Jarrod Shusterman.**

Don't worry about understanding everything; just try to understand the main ideas in the story.

DAY ONE
SATURDAY, JUNE 4TH

The kitchen faucet makes the most bizarre sounds.

It coughs and wheezes like it's gone asthmatic. It gurgles like someone drowning. It spits once, and then goes silent. Our dog, Kingston, raises his ears, but still keeps his distance from the sink, unsure if it might unexpectedly come back to life, but no such luck.

Mom just stands there holding Kingston's water bowl beneath the faucet, puzzling. Then she moves the handle to the off position, and says, "Alyssa, go get your father." [...]

"Dad," I shouted out into the garage, "kitchen issues."

My father's feet stick out from underneath his Camry like the Wicked Witch. [...]

"Can't it wait?" my Dad says from beneath the car.

But I'm already sensing that it can't. "I think it's major," I tell him.

He slides out, and with a heavy sigh heads for the kitchen.

Mom's not there anymore. Instead she is standing in the doorway between the kitchen and the living room. She's just standing there, the dog's empty water bowl still in her left hand. I get a chill, but I don't yet know why.

"What's so important that you gotta drag me out of ---"

"Shush!" Mom says. She rarely shushes Dad. She'll shush me and Garrett all day, but my parents never shush each other. It's an unspoken rule.

She's watching TV, where a news presenter is blathering about the "flow crisis." That's what the media's been calling the drought, ever since people got tired of hearing the word "drought." Kind of like the way "global warming" became "climate change," and "war" became "conflict." But now they've got a new catchphrase. A new stage in our water problems. They're calling this the "Tap-Out."

Uncle Basil [...] asks, "What's going on?"

"Arizona and Nevada just backed out of the water program," Mom tells him. "They won't give us anymore water, saying they need the water themselves."

Which means that the Colorado River won't even reach California anymore.

Uncle Basil tries to wrap his mind around it. "Turning off the entire river like a faucet! Can they do that?"

My father raises an eyebrow. "They just did."

Suddenly the image switches to a live press conference, where the governor addresses a gathering of nervous reporters.

"This is unfortunate, but not entirely unexpected," the governor says. "We have people working around the clock attempting to broker a new deal with various companies."

"What does that even mean?" Uncle Basil says. Both Mom and I shush him. [...]

"But I cannot stress enough the need to keep calm. I'd like to personally assure everyone that this is a temporary situation, and that there is nothing to be concerned about." [...]

I go to the kitchen to try the tap myself – as if I might have the magic touch. Nothing. Not even the slightest dribble. [...] I note the time, like they do in the emergency room: 1:32 p.m., June 4th.

Everyone's going to remember where they were when the taps went dry, I think.

43/8 **2 Answer the questions. Write the lines in the story where you found the answers. Write short answers.**

1. Who is the narrator of the story?

2. What is Alyssa's dad doing in the garage?

3. What is the "Tap-Out" and what caused it?

4. What does the governor say on TV? (3 details)

5. Why is the last sentence in italics?

43/8 **3 Look at the text. What do the following words mean? Match the words (A–J) as used in the text with their definitions. Write the correct numbers in the grid below.**

A faucet or tap (line 1)
B gurgle (line 4)
C slide (line 22)
D chill (line 28)
E drag (line 29)
F shush (line 31)
G blather (line 36)
H catchphrase (line 42)
I wrap around (line 51)
J dribble (line 71)

1. well-known words
2. a few drops of water
3. to try to understand something
4. to make a strange sound
5. to tell someone to be quiet
6. to pull something or someone
7. the feeling of being cold
8. the metal thing where water comes out in kitchens and bathrooms
9. to move smoothly out from under something
10. to talk in an annoying way

Some words sound like their meaning when you say them out loud or they're smiliar to the German word.

A	B	C	D	E	F	G	H	I	J

43/8 **4 (WRITING) Have you ever experienced a major crisis, something that affected your whole town or even country? How did you feel? What happened?**

How did people react? How did the situation end? Write 200 words about it in your exercise book.

These words may help you:

flood, snow, fire, thunderstorm, attack
terrified, alone, surprised, shocked, worried

44/2

1 Mind maps

a) Look at the texts in your book on pages 44–45. Use words from the texts to finish the mind map.

b) Now make more mind maps in your exercise book using the following words: healthcare, pandemic and factory. When you have finished using words from the texts, you can add your own words.

7
46/5

2 Listen to four young people talk about how they like to communicate.

a) Listen to the interviews and write down four facts about each person.

1. Isabella: ______________________________

2. James: ______________________________

3. Sophia: ______________________________

4. Thomas: ______________________________

b) Fill in the missing words about the four people.

1. Isabella has *discussions* with her friends. She feels strongly about some issues and takes part in ______________.
2. James enjoys discussions with people who ______________ his opinions. He only ______________ everyone to stay calm and sensible.
3. Sophie expresses her opinion in her ______________. She sometimes gets ______________ posts.
4. Thomas expresses his opinion in his ______________ slogans. He doesn't want to ______________ his art to other people.

46/6 ↗ **3** **Fill in the missing words. Use all the words in blue at least once.**

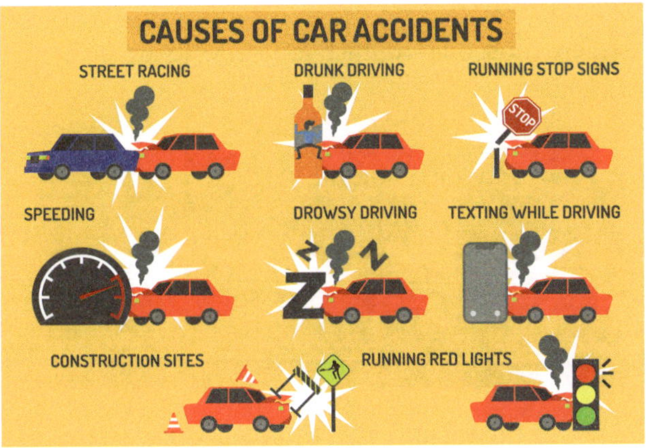

might | must (not) | have to | should (not) | cannot | not allowed to

1. You cannot race in the streets.
2. You ______ drink before you drive.
3. You ______ stop at stop signs.
4. You are ______ speed.
5. You ______ drive while tired.
6. You ______ have an accident if you text while driving.
7. You ______ be careful when driving through a construction site.
8. You are ______ run a red light.

46/7 ↗ **4** **Write sentences about the pictures in the past tense using "should" and "shouldn't".**

These words might help:

manhole
banana
while crossing the busy street
curtain
pay attention
front door

1. He should not have been talking on his phone near a manhole.
2. Someone ______
3. ______
4. ______
5. ______
6. ______

47/9 **5** (MEDIATION) **Verwende die Informationen über Demonstrationen und bearbeite die Aufgaben stichpunktartig auf Deutsch.**

Es ist keine wörtliche Übersetzung nötig, die Aspekte müssen inhaltlich jedoch vollständig erfasst sein. Einzelwörter genügen nicht als Antwort.

Arizona, USA

London, England

All over the world more and more people are taking to the streets to protest about social, political and ecological problems, from Hong Kong to Russia and from Chile to France. There are national political demonstrations against corruption in the government or the economy; there are local protests about the construction of a new airport, the lack of public transport – or the destruction of a woodland area.

In the past few years there has not only been an increase in worldwide protests but also a change in the focus. Protesters see all these ills and threats as interconnected in one huge global complex. The unfair distribution of wealth means that millions are poor, the exploitation of nature causes water pollution and land becomes unsuitable for agriculture.

An ever-increasing number of protesters are teenagers and young adults. They are angry and impatient with the way the older generations have used their power to exploit resources but have failed so far to manage serious global or regional problems. It is no wonder that the younger generation worldwide is united in anger about a situation which will probably ruin their future, although it is in no way their fault.

Taking part in a protest often means walking peacefully through a town. But in some countries people risk their lives to take part in a demonstration against the establishment. Videos of violent police actions against peaceful demonstrators are familiar to all of us, even in countries which uphold the Human Rights Act that guarantees the right to free speech and peaceful protest.

It is important for demonstrators to take some precautions. First of all, check the people organising the demonstration and the subject of the protest. You want to know who you are marching with. Then there are a few practical considerations. Be prepared for a long walk, maybe in unfavourable weather. Take some food and water. Know your rights and check out what rights the police have. There are many useful websites on "How to stay safe at demonstrations".

1. Wogegen wird auf nationaler Ebene protestiert?

2. Was hat sich in den letzten Jahren geändert? (2 Dinge)

3. Was vereint die jüngere Generation weltweit?

4. Was ist die erste Vorsichtsmaßnahme, die Demonstranten vor einer Demo ergreifen sollten?

50/8 ## 1 Read the text about in-person communication.

Everywhere we go, we see people communicating with each other, either visually or orally or both. It's so easy to send a text – with or without a photo – to a friend. (1) With a phone call or voicemail you can feel a bit closer to the person and maybe guess their mood. (Surprised? Angry?) Then there's the digital combination of both – the video link. (2)

Do all these technical possibilities mean that in-person communication is inferior or even unnecessary? No way! (3) That is why there are still so many conferences around the world. People still want to be near each other and not just see people in pictures or on phones. Here are some of the reasons why. (4) The partners can react to each other's emotions more quickly and misunderstandings are less likely. Furthermore, speakers can tell at once when they don't have their partner's full attention.

(5) A real partner can't be switched off! (6) There's also the whole sphere of body language, another important form of communication. (7) Your conversation is safe from any spies in the digital world of social media and online shopping!

a) Look at the text again. Five sentences have been removed from the text. Choose the correct gap (1–7) in the text for each of the sentences below (A–E). Write the correct number of the gap behind each sentence. Be careful: There are two gaps which you do not need to use.

A With in-person communication it's not just a question of someone's face and voice. ☐

B There is nothing like face-to-face contact. ☐

C One final advantage of face-to-face communication: privacy. ☐

D First of all, no video camera can replace the direct contact with a real person. ☐

E This is much faster and more efficient than a traditional phone call. ☐

8 b) You will hear five statements by teenagers about communicating. How can you describe them based on their favourite way of communicating? Write the correct numbers (1–5) in the boxes next to the categories (A–H). Be careful: Use each number only once.

A a player	☐	E a fan of the landline	☐
B a traditionalist	☐	F a blogger	☐
C an organiser	☐	G a video camera girl	☐
D an all-rounder	☐	H a texter	☐

c) What is the best way to communicate? Write your opinion.

___

___

___

Lösungen online
8qy4zy

___/6P

1 I can understand information about the world.

→p. 34/1

The paragraphs of the text are mixed up. Put the parts (A–F) into the right order (1–6).

A Speaking of water, everyone knows that water covers 71 % of our planet's surface. But did you know that less than 1 % is available for us to drink?
B That must be quite a shock for the sun-loving camels. Furthermore, snow is not completely unknown in the Arabian desert. The last real snowfall there was in January 2020. By the way, if you want to experience a desert, with or without snow, you'll have to travel some way. Europe is the only continent without any deserts.
C Geography quizzes are very popular with all age groups, especially if the questions are not too difficult. So let's start with an easy one. Which is the highest mountain in the world? We said it was an easy one; it's Mount Everest (8,840 metres).
D Some countries have a problem with rivers. They simply don't have any. Saudi Arabia is the biggest country without any permanent rivers. The land is mainly desert, not only dry but very hot too, except during some winter nights, when the temperature can go down to 4 °C.
E The rest contains too much salt and other substances, or it's locked up in glaciers and snowfields. That just shows how important our freshwater lakes and rivers are.
F Really? That depends on where you start measuring from. If you start at sea level, then no mountain is higher than Everest. But if you include the depth of the ocean, then Mauna Kea on the island of Hawaii is the highest: a total of more than 10,000 metres, above and below sea level. And most of the mountain is under water.

A	B	C	D	E	F

___/8P

2 I can describe the pros and cons of a technological development.

→p. 34/2
9

Listen to the report about a clever modern invention. Describe the C-pen reader in one sentence.

It's a pen which ______________________________.

Make notes about the advantages and the disadvantages of the invention.

ADVANTAGES	DISADVANTAGES
• ______	• ______
• ______	• ______
______	• ______
• ______	• ______
• ______	
• ______	

___/3P 3 I can understand a speech about water.

→p. 35/3

Read paragraphs E–H of the text "Water, water everywhere?" on page 41 in your book again. Tick the correct answers. There may be more than one.

1. Water is used inefficiently because …
   a) there is an unfair price system. ☐
   b) wastage is not punished. ☐
   c) there are not enough lakes. ☐
2. Water pollution must be prevented by …
   a) reducing the number of fish caught. ☐
   b) punishing the polluters. ☐
   c) using the latest technology. ☐
3. Climate change has serious negative effects, for example …
   a) power stations use up too much water. ☐
   b) planning for the future is more difficult. ☐
   c) droughts and floods. ☐

___/4P 4 I can write an online comment.

→p. 35/4

Look back at the story on page 26 in this workbook. Imagine you are Alyssa and you have just heard the governor's speech on TV. You decide to write an online comment to the governor's office. Write Alyssa's online comment.

____

____

____

____

____

___/3P 5 I can understand a report about a conference.

→p. 35/5

Read this text about a youth congress. Then answer the questions in note form.

The World Youth Congress brings together youth leaders from around the world. The annual weekend congress is held in a different country every time. Previous hosts have included Istanbul, Rio de Janeiro, and Hawaii. The exact topic of the congress changes from year to year, but the focus is always on sustainability, justice for everyone worldwide and a better future for our planet. Some years ago the main topic at the World Youth Congress in Rio was water resources. The delegates demanded action from governments against pollution, exploitation and the degradation of our oceans.
Every year more than 100 youth leaders take part in discussions and events where they can make plans for future activities in their special field.

1. What key facts do you find out about the organisation of the congress? (Who? Where?)
   ____
2. What topics are discussed? ______________________________

Lösungen online
8qy4zy

○ 1 I can understand information about the world.

Look at the texts about a global village in your book on pages 34–35 again. Are these sentences true (T), false (F) or is the information not in the texts (N)?

	T	F	N
1. Most people in the world are not older than 35.	☐	☐	☐
2. Most people in the world have a car.	☐	☐	☐
3. The richest people in the world live in rich countries.	☐	☐	☐
4. People speak thousands of different languages.	☐	☐	☐
5. Most people speak English.	☐	☐	☐
6. Girls go to school less than boys.	☐	☐	☐
7. Not many people work in agriculture anymore.	☐	☐	☐
8. Most people in the world are not overweight.	☐	☐	☐

○ 2 I can describe the pros and cons of a technological development.

Digital touchscreens are very popular in business and in education. Now digital tables go a few steps further than whiteboards. The screen is not vertical. It is horizontal like a dining table and everyone can sit or stand around it. This means that there isn't just one person operating the screen and very often not even looking at the listeners. With a digital table, everyone has the same access to the screen on the table and no one has to read anything upside down. But the quality of the visuals depends very much on the lighting. If there is a lot of daylight or the wrong kind of artificial light, then the screen is not easy to read.

Having just one digital table for all means that participants don't need their own laptops or phones, so everyone concentrates better. But there is a limit to the number of people who can take part round the tabletop. And compared with a whiteboard, a digital table is extremely expensive. Still, for those companies that can afford it, a digital table provides direct and effective communication.

List the pros and cons of this technical development in the table.

PROS	CONS
• ______________	• ______________
• ______________	• ______________
• ______________	• ______________
• ______________	
• ______________	

○ 3 I can understand a speech about water.

Read the text on pages 40–41 in your textbook again. Finish the sentences with information from the right paragraph in the text.

Paragraph A: We can improve public health and reduce poverty if we can develop ____________________, ____________________ and ____________________.

Paragraph D: Efforts to develop water access and reduce poverty are threatened by ____________________ ____________________.

Paragraph G: Water waste can be reduced in two ways: by ____________________ pay and by ____________________ innovations.

○ 4 I can write an online comment. Write about 60 words.

Someone has posted a photo of a beach near your house online. You decide to write a comment about it online. You can use the words in the boxes below to help you.

awful	thoughtless	ruin
garbage	dirty	dangerous

____

____

____

____

○ 5 I can understand a report about a conference.

The World Youth Congress brings young leaders together to discuss a better future for our planet. The annual weekend congress is held in a different country every time. The focus is always on a particular aspect of sustainability worldwide. Each delegate then returns to his or her country to pass on the message of the Congress.

The Youth Sports Leaders' Conference takes place in Baltimore this year. It is open to people who are involved with children's sport as coaches or trainers. Participants listen to talks from experts, discuss new developments in sports education and take part in practical training sessions with experienced coaches.

At this year's Online Safety Conference, the focus will be on the youth. Participants will discuss how young people can learn to deal with fake news and with the upsetting or illegal content which sometimes pops up during games. There will be presentations by experts followed by discussions and workshops.

Which of these three conferences would you like to attend? Why? Give at least three reasons.

____

____

WRITING SKILLS

Here you can learn how to write a story.

55/3 **1 You want to take part in an English writing competition about the environment. Write about 200 words.**

a) Here are some tips to help you write your story:

	You can write your own ideas for your story here and in your exercise book.
Do you need ideas for your story? Then think about things that have happened to you, or books you have read or films you have seen. For example, think about the story you read on page 26. Don't forget to write a suitable beginning to your story.	*For example, you could write a story about a protest, like the story on page 37.*
Think about who is telling the story. Are you the narrator or someone else telling the story?	*For example, you could be the narrator, like the story on page 37.*
Who are the characters in your story? What are these characters like? Are they like people you know in real life?	*For example, Morton and Livia are the main characters in the story on page 37.*
Think about where your story takes place: in a forest, a city or a spaceship.	*For example, the story can happen in a town called Newton, like in the story on page 37.*
Have you been told when the story takes place?	*Note: This information may be given to you if you have to write a story in your final exam.*
Plan the plot of your story. Do you want to start by introducing your main character or with an interesting event? Think about the main idea in your story. Is there a problem that has to be solved or does something funny or surprising happen?	*For example, the problem is that Livia is going to make them very late in the story on page 37.*
How will you end your story? Do you find a solution to the problem or does the story have an open ending? Write a suitable ending to your story.	*For example, the story on page 37 has an open ending.*

b) Read the following introduction to a story.

In Newton feelings were running very high because there were plans for a new factory on the edge of the town. To make room for it, an area of woodland would have to be cut down. Thousands of people were very much against this project and had already organised online petitions and demonstrations. Now there were plans for a big protest march from the town hall to the woodland area. It was going to start from the town hall at eleven o'clock on Saturday morning. Morton and his girlfriend Livia were going to take part.
"I'll call you at quarter to eleven," Morton said to Livia. "OK," she said, "I'll make a cool banner – a really big one!"
Saturday morning came. Livia was woken up at nine o'clock when her phone rang. Her friend Samantha had sent her information about the new factory. Livia was horrified. It seemed that the damage to the environment was going to be even worse than they'd feared. She followed one link after another ...
Suddenly Livia heard the doorbell ring. Quarter to eleven! It was Morton. "I forgot the time. – I'm not even dressed yet!" Livia called out to him.
"Well, hurry up!" Morton said impatiently. "Just get on any old clothes. Let's see your cool banner!"
Livia's heart sank. "I'm so sorry. It just says 'STOP' and 'NO'. I didn't get any further. But the main thing is that we're part of the march!"

c) Now write your own story. Include the following aspects: a threat to the environment, a fight between friends, an emotional moment and a surprise.

Lösungen online
8qy4zy

Future, here we come!

57/6 **1** **Complete the second sentence so that it has a similar meaning to the first sentence, using the KEY WORD given in brackets.**

Do not change the KEY WORD given. You must use between two and five words including the KEY WORD.

1. New York City hosts the famous week-long World Science Festival every year. (BY)

   Every year the famous week-long World Science Festival ______________________________ New York City.

2. The goal of the festival is to make science accessible and exciting for the general public. (SUCCEED)

   The festival ______________________________ making science accessible and exciting for the general public.

3. Brian Greene, a co-founder of the festival, is a scientist who tries to teach everyone about science by writing books, giving talks and hosting TV shows. (ORDER)

   ______________________________ about science, Brian Greene, a co-founder of the festival, writes books, gives talks and hosts TV shows.

4. Many famous actors and scientists dream of taking part in events at the festival. (WISHED)

   Many famous actors and scientists ______________________________ in events at the festival.

5. The festival brings science to people around the world through films, theater, discussions and hands-on experiments. (USED)

   Films, theater, discussions and hands-on experiments ______________________________ science to people around the world.

6. The festival was so popular in New York City that there is now a similar festival in Brisbane, Australia. (DUE)

   ______________________________ in New York City, there is now a similar festival in Brisbane, Australia.

7. You don't have to go to New York City to take part in the festival; millions of people watch it online every year. (INSTEAD)

   ______________________________ New York City to take part in the festival, you can watch it online.

57/6 **2** **(WRITING) Emma writes an e-mail to her friends asking them to join her at her house to watch some of the World Science Festival online.**

Write Emma's invitation in your exercise book. Find a suitable beginning and ending. Write about 200 words.

Tell them:
- why the festival is a great idea
- who is going to be there
- what kind of events there are
- where and when you are meeting

57/6

3 (SPEAKING) Alice, a high school student in New York City, is talking to Jennifer Jones, a scientist and guest speaker at the World Science Festival in New York.

Cover your partner's part of the dialogue with a piece of paper, but don't cover the arrows (→). Then act out the dialogue with your partner.

Alice

1. Sage hallo und wie du heißt. Du bist sehr froh, sie kennenzulernen. Ihre Rede bei dem Festival hat dir sehr gefallen.
2. *Hello Alice. Thank you so much and please call me Jennifer. Did you enjoy the festival?*
3. Ja. Du freust dich schon auf nächstes Jahr. Du weißt, dass sie eine Physikerin ist, aber du fragst, seit wann sie sich für Wissenschaft interessiert.
4. *Oh, when I was very young. I wanted to find out where everything came from and how everything worked. And I still do!*
5. Du auch! Frage sie, woran sie gerade arbeitet.
6. *At the moment I am studying black holes and the role they play in our galaxy. What science projects have you worked on?*
7. Sage, dass du im Moment einen Roboter im Physikunterricht baust und dass es ziemlich cool ist.
8. *Will you send me a picture of it when you're done? And I'll send you a copy of my latest book on black holes.*
9. Sage, klar, das machst du gerne und vielen Dank!

Jennifer

1. *Hello Ms Jones. My name is Alice and it's so great to meet you. I loved your talk at the science festival.*
2. Sage hallo und vielen Dank. Sie soll dich Jennifer nennen. Frage, ob ihr das Festival gefallen hat.
3. *Yes, I can't wait to come back next year. I know you're a physicist, but when did you first become interested in science?*
4. Seit du sehr klein bist. Du wolltest wissen, woher alles kommt und wie alles funktioniert. Und das willst du immer noch!
5. *Me too! What are you working on right now?*
6. Sage, dass du im Moment schwarze Löcher und ihre Rolle in der Galaxie erforschst. Frage sie, an welchen wissenschaftlichen Projekten sie gearbeitet hat.
7. *Right now we are building a robot in our physics class. It's pretty cool.*
8. Frage, ob sie dir ein Foto schickt, wenn er fertig ist. Dann schickst du ihr eine Kopie deines letzten Buches über schwarze Löcher.
9. *Sure, I'd love to and thanks!*

Noughts & Crosses

67/13 1 **Read the text about the book *Noughts & Crosses* and answer the questions.**

Callum is a nought (0), a white citizen, in a society controlled by black Crosses. The noughts are called 'Blankers' as a racist insult by the Crosses, suggesting that they are a worthless waste of space.

Sephy is a Cross (X), and the daughter of one of the most powerful politicians in the country. She lives a life of luxury and privilege.

Sephy and Callum take turns telling the story of their childhood friendship turning into love. They try to find a way to be together, but society is against them.

The book *Noughts & Crosses* by Malorie Blackman has now been made into a major BBC TV series.

1. Why do you think the noughts are written with a small letter 'n' and the Crosses with a capital 'C'?

2. How is society in the book different to real life? Why do you think the writer chose to do this?

10 67/13 2 **The noughts and Crosses society**

You will hear five statements about the noughts and Crosses society. What aspects of the society are being talked about? Write the correct numbers (1–5) in the boxes next to the categories (A–H). Be careful: Use each number only once.

A	Fashion	☐	E	Goods	☐
B	Media	☐	F	Government	☐
C	School	☐	G	Books	☐
D	Religion	☐	H	Homes	☐

67/13

3 *Noughts & Crosses:* Callum

a) The Cross government is now allowing some noughts to go to Cross schools. Callum has worked very hard to get into the Cross school, Heathcroft. He really wants to go there because Cross schools are better than nought schools. Read Callum's text about the talk he has with his mum the night before he starts at his new school.

Mum came into the room, carefully shutting the door behind her. I could guess what was about to come next. She sat on my bed, picked up my school bag and immediately emptied everything out. Very carefully, Mum started packing all my stuff back. Moments passed before she spoke. 'I just wanted to say that whatever happens tomorrow, well done for getting into Heathcroft High.'

That I hadn't expected. I stared at her.

'What d'you mean, whatever happens tomorrow?'

'Nothing.' Mum's smile wobbled before disappearing altogether. 'It's just that ... that I want you to be happy.'

'I am happy.' I frowned.

'I don't want to see you ... upset. I don't want you to get hurt.'

What on earth was she talking about? 'Mum, I'm only going to school. I'm not going into the army!'

Mum's attempt at a smile was back. 'I know. But I think you and your father are underestimating how much of a ... challenge it's going to be. I don't want to see you upset. Besides which ... well, we've heard some rumours ...'

'Some of the Crosses aren't happy about noughts going to their schools. We've heard rumours that some of them are determined to cause trouble. So, no matter what happens, don't let yourself be provoked into lashing out. Don't give them a reason to kick you out.'

'Is that what you've been worrying about?'

Mum didn't reply.

'Don't worry,' I told her. 'I've got into Heathcroft now and nothing, not even dynamite, is going to get me out again.'

b) Look at the text. Find a word or expression which means the same as each of the words (1–8) below. The lines where you can find the words or expressions are indicated in brackets.

1. to close → ______________________ (lines 1–3)
2. to raise → ______________________ (lines 4–6)
3. to hope for → ______________________ (lines 10–12)
4. to shake → ______________________ (lines 13–15)
5. to look sad or angry → ______________________ (lines 15–18)
6. a struggle → ______________________ (lines 19–21)
7. to undervalue → ______________________ (lines 19–21)
8. to excite → ______________________ (lines 22–24)

67/13

4 *Noughts & Crosses: Sephy*

a) Today is Callum's first day at Sephy's school, Heathcroft. Sephy is really excited that Callum is going to go to her school. Read Sephy's text about what happens in front of her school on Callum's first day.

As I approached the corner, shouts like an angry wave rolled up towards me. But even that couldn't prepare me for what was about to happen next.
I turned the corner and …
And.
At the far end of the road, there was a huge crowd outside my school. And they were shouting and chanting. I froze for a moment, then started to walk towards them. Then I started to run. What on earth was going on? It didn't take me long to find out.
'NO BLANKERS IN OUR SCHOOL.
NO BLANKERS IN OUR SCHOOL.'
The slogan was shouted out over and over again. Callum and three other noughts were surrounded by police officers who were trying to push their way through the crowd to get to the school entrance. More police stood in an arm-linked line trying to push the crowd of Crosses back into two orderly groups. I ran faster, but the closer I got, the less I could see.
I pushed and elbowed my way through the crowd.
'Callum! Callum!'
'NO BLANKERS IN OUR SCHOOL. …'
The police officers were trying to push through the crowds of adults and Heathcroft pupils who in turn were determined not to let them pass.

b) Look at the text. What do the following words mean? Match the expressions (A–H) as used in the text with their corresponding definitions (1–10). Write the correct numbers in the grid below. Be careful: There are two definitions that you do not need.

A to approach (line 1)
B huge (line 6)
C to chant (line 8)
D to freeze (line 8)
E to surround (line 14)
F line (line 15)
G to elbow (line 17)
H determined (line 21)

1. to stand very still
2. to have no space
3. to force your way through
4. to come near to
5. to do with purpose
6. a piece of rope
7. to repeat words again and again
8. people standing next to each other
9. to become very cold
10. very large

A	B	C	D	E	F	G	H

67/13

5 *Noughts & Crosses:* Sephy and Callum

a) Read the extracts again and answer the questions.

1. Where is the first text set? How do you know?
   ____
2. What has Callum's mum heard rumours about?
   ____
   ____
3. What does she think Callum might do?
   ____
4. How does Sephy first find out about the protestors?
   ____
5. What are the people protesting about?
   ____
6. Why do you think Sephy 'froze'?
   ____

b) How do you think the people are feeling in the texts? Think of an adjective for each of these people. Why do you think they feel like that? These words can help you: scared, worried, upset, angry or determined.

Text: Callum

Callum might feel __________ because ______________________

____

Callum's mum might feel __________ because ______________________

____

Text: Sephy

Sephy might feel __________ because ______________________

____

Callum might feel __________ because ______________________

____

The protestors might feel __________ because ______________________

____

c) Discuss these questions in a group.

1. How did you feel on the first day before starting school? Why did you feel like that?
2. Have you ever been to a protest? If so, what was it for and why did you go?
   If not, would you ever go to one and what for?
3. Can you think of a time when something happened to another person that made you feel angry or upset? Tell your group what happened and what you did.

67/13 6 (WRITING) *Noughts & Crosses:* Sephy and Callum

a) Imagine Callum and Sephy meet in front of the school after the protest. What would they say to each other? How do they feel? Do they have the same opinions about the protest? What do they want to do next? Write a dialogue between Sephy and Callum. Write about 200 words. Then act out your dialogue with a partner.

OR

Imagine that you were a reporter in front of Heathcroft's entrance on Callum's first day and that you talked to Callum and Sephy. What would you write about the events? Write 200 words. Include information about the number of people who were involved, statements from two different people, what caused the event and how it ended. Then read your report to your partner.

● b) Imagine Callum was able to start school that day. What do you think his first day was like? Pretend you are Callum and write about your first day at your new school. Write about 200 words in your exercise book.

11 67/13

7 A review of the BBC series *Noughts & Crosses*

You will hear a review on the radio of the BBC series *Noughts & Crosses*. There are six wrong words in the text. Underline them and write the correct version on the lines provided.

This BBC series has been adopted from Malorie Blackman's novel *Noughts & Crosses*. It is set in the imaginary country of 'Albion', where light-skinned noughts are controlled by the darker skinned Crosses, who colonized Europe hundreds of years ago from 'Aprica'. The African influence in the series is strong. The architecture has an African style, the clothes choose African fabrics and even the white characters in the series have African hairstyles. This celebration of Africa is continued in the music, which features many African musicians. The idea of turning society around is cleverly shown. Here, people pronounce right people's names wrong, university lecturers and TV presenters are black, and white people struggle to escape properly.

Fans of the book will notice a few changes. Although the main idea of a nought boy, Callum, and a rich Cross girl, Sephy, falling in love and the problems that creates for them and their families is the fame, in the series the characters are older. Now, Callum is not one of the first noughts to go to a Cross high school, but one of the first noughts to join the military academy.

Sometimes this six-part series feels a little rushed, and the characters should have been given more time to develop themselves and their relationships. However, it is an interesting and important piece of television.

International work and trade

69/3 **1 Complete the sentences about globalisation. Use the correct form of the verbs.**

accounting | banking | wages | devastated | freelance | outsource | parcels | pollution | a number of | redundant | sick pay | deliver

1. Large container ships bring goods to the ports, then thousands of ____________ are ____________ to customers.
2. Employees and ____________ workers often travel abroad to work on ____________ projects.
3. A good education is necessary to get a job with good ____________ and other benefits such as ____________.
4. People feel ____________ when the only earner in the family is made ____________ and all their lives change.
5. Companies often ____________ production to poorer countries.
6. More and more people are exposed to ____________ and climate change.
7. The global ____________ industry is concentrated in a few financial centres and many people are needed who are skilled in ____________.

69/3 **2 Which aspect of globalisation do you think will affect your life the most in the future?**

Together with your partner you must prepare a presentation about globalisation. Talk about the different aspects shown in the pictures and then decide on the two aspects you want to focus on in your presentation.

12 71/5

1 Listen to the text about parks in Hong Kong. Tick the right answer.

1. Malcolm is from …
   a) Hong Kong. ☐
   b) New York. ☐
   c) London. ☐
   d) China. ☐

2. One problem in Hong Kong is …
   a) the high rents. ☐
   b) there are not enough parks. ☐
   c) the high buildings. ☐
   d) there are too many businesses. ☐

3. Kowloon Park is …
   a) a shopping mall. ☐
   b) a nature reserve. ☐
   c) on an island. ☐
   d) on the mainland. ☐

4. Kowloon Park also has …
   a) a skate park. ☐
   b) a swimming pool. ☐
   c) traditional Chinese buildings. ☐
   d) skyscrapers. ☐

5. Malcolm's daughter loves ...
   a) Hong Kong. ☐
   b) swimming. ☐
   c) skateboarding. ☐
   d) parks. ☐

6. Mei Foo skate park is…
   a) on top of a building. ☐
   b) expensive to visit. ☐
   c) brand new. ☐
   d) a good place for beginners. ☐

7. Nan Lian Gardens …
   a) is on an island. ☐
   b) doesn't have many trees. ☐
   c) has many Chinese features. ☐
   d) is popular with sports fans. ☐

8. Victoria park is …
   a) on the mainland. ☐
   b) a place for quiet relaxation. ☐
   c) a place for public events. ☐
   d) famous for its lakes and wildlife. ☐

72/6 2 Choose the right tense: simple present or present progressive?

1. David Cheng is a software expert who ____________ (work) for an international bank in Kowloon.
2. At home with his parents he ____________ (speak) Cantonese, but he ____________ (do) all his banking work in English.
3. It's Sunday evening and David's mother ____________ (prepare) a meal in the small kitchen.
4. She always ____________(manage) to cook tasty food.
5. David ____________ (look) closely at his phone. He ____________ (search) online for a room of his own.
6. He ____________ (check) the offers every day, but he never ____________ (find) anything he can afford.

72/7 3 Complete the text using the correct tense in the past.

The Wang family (1) ____________ (sell) goods at their Hong Kong market stall for the past thirty years. To begin with, Mr Wang (2) ____________ (sell) cheap clothing to the people of Hong Kong. Then he (3) ____________ (notice) that more and more foreign tourists (4) ____________ (go) to the market. So he (5) ____________ (decide) to sell clothes with traditional Chinese designs. As a child Mr Wang's son Tony (6) ____________ (not have) much free time because he (7) ____________ (help) his parents. Two years ago Tony (8) ____________ (take over) from his father. Since then Tony (9) ____________ (have) even less time – and some unpleasant experiences. While he (10) ____________ (talk) to a customer yesterday, a thief (11) ____________ (steal) a Chinese jacket. "I (12) ____________ (not be able) to get it back yet," Tony says, "but it (13) ____________ (be) an expensive one."

73/9

4 (MEDIATION) Verwende die Informationen über Lebensverhältnisse in Hong Kong und bearbeite die Aufgaben (1–6) stichpunktartig auf Deutsch.

Es ist keine wörtliche Übersetzung nötig, die Aspekte müssen inhaltlich jedoch vollständig erfasst sein. Einzelwörter genügen nicht als Antwort.

Hong Kong is a city of contrasts and contradictions. There are more super-rich people in Hong Kong than anywhere else in the world. The rich use their money both to invest and to consume. As a result the Hong Kong property market is the most expensive in the world. Hong Kong also has one of the most exclusive retail districts worldwide. All the luxury brands are there, from perfume to cars. One reason for the high property prices is the fact that land for building is very scarce in Hong Kong. It is a small territory anyway and much of the land is very hilly and unsuitable for building. Of course, the wealthy choose the best places to live – luxury apartments and large villas with spectacular views over Hong Kong harbour.
And what about the people with less money? They crowd into the rest of the living accommodation, usually in cramped, high-rise buildings. Rents are high and wages are low, so the poorest residents have to take what they can get. It is estimated that at least 200,000 people live in tiny containers, known as "cages", which measure about 1.5 square metres and cost up to 200 US dollars rent a month. A "normal" room in an apartment can be divided into 20 – 30 of these cages. This form of sub-letting is illegal, but it is still very common. The government has plans to create more homes for the poorer residents, but land is often sold to investors who prefer to build luxury accommodation.
Social conflict is growing in Hong Kong, not only for political reasons. Many people are frustrated because they see no way of escaping from their economic and social problems.

1. Was machen die reichen Bewohner Hong Kongs mit ihrem Geld? ______
2. Warum sind Immobilien so teuer? ______
3. Wo wohnen die meisten Einwohner? ______
4. Was sind „cages"? ______
5. Welche Rolle spielt die Regierung? ______
6. Wie wirkt sich der Gegensatz zwischen Armen und Reichen aus? Nenne 2 Details. ______

73/9

5 (SPEAKING) Compare the two photos above.

Think about what you read in the text. Then talk to your group about the photos.

More about Miguel

Miguel and his son Luis have good reason to look happy.

They used to live in rented accommodation, but two years ago they bought their own small house. **(1)** When Miguel was a child, he left school at the age of 15. **(2)** Like all the youngsters of his age he started working on the banana plantation. He didn't earn very much and his family was very poor. **(3)**

But thanks to Fairtrade the situation for Miguel's family is much better. The bananas are now sold directly to the Fairtrade company, which pays the cooperative a premium. **(4)** The school which Luis (14) attends has received funds from Fairtrade projects.

The money has been used for books, computers and IT training. **(5)** The school has recently bought some new sports equipment, which the students can use in their spare time. **(6)** Luis and his friends play football and basketball, and they enjoy watching big games on TV. Unfortunately, many teenagers drop out of school before they finish their education. **(7)** "It would be wonderful to have a doctor in the family," Miguel says.

75/4

1 Read the text above about Miguel and his family.

Five sentences have been removed from the text. Choose the correct gap (1–7) in the text for each of the sentences below (A–E). Write the correct number of the gap behind each sentence. Be careful: There are two gaps which you do not need to use.

A Digital skills are important for the students' future. ☐

B There was no free medical care and working conditions were insecure. ☐

C But Luis is determined to do well at school and study medicine at university. ☐

D All the farmers in the cooperative decide together how this money is to be spent. ☐

E They managed this with the help of money from Fairtrade. ☐

75/4

2 Look at the text again.

Find a word or expression which means the same as each of the words (1–5) below.

1. housing → ____________________
2. to make money → ____________________
3. not long ago → ____________________
4. to leave early / too soon → ____________________
5. great → ____________________

77/5

1 Read the customer reviews of Re-stitched.

Complete the sentences with the words in the boxes. (Choose blue for the first paragraph, orange for the second paragraph and green for the third paragraph.) There are more words than you need. Use the correct form.

compress · cotton · cushions · fabric · upcycle · thrilled · sustainable

cupboard · damage · donates · handbags · launched · refashioned

jumper · ever-shorter · thread · tights · toxic · touch · linen · vegan

I'm (1) ______ with my new (2) ______ ! What a good idea to (3) ______ jeans! The (4) ______ probably isn't organic, but recycled stuff is (5) ______ nevertheless. I'll be looking at your website regularly from now on! *Marsha Simmons*

My girlfriend has so many (6) ______ in her (7) ______ that she (8) ______ some to the charity shop every year. But when she saw this one, (9) ______ from a jacket, she had to have it – for her dog, which she takes everywhere. I guess she has (10) ______ a new fashion in animal transport! *Carl Sanchez*

I can't believe that my new hat was once a (11) ______ ! It's so warm and soft to (12) ______ , and the style is classic. I hate today's (13) ______ fashion seasons, so I try not to buy many new clothes and certainly not any fabrics with (14) ______ chemicals. Next summer I'll be looking for one of your tops made from old (15) ______ ! Keep up the good work! *Harriet Turner*

2 (SPEAKING) What kind of clothes do you buy?

77/5

Do you know where they are made? How often do you wear the clothes you buy? Can you imagine buying upcycled clothes? Take notes and then talk to a partner about it.

______

______

______

77/6 ## 3 Complete the text with a suitable form of the passive.

In the past most of our clothes (1) ______________ (make) in Europe. Then production (2) ______________ ______________ (slowly move) to other places. Today clothes (3) ______________ (can, produce) very cheaply in some countries because wages are so low. As a result, individual pieces of clothing (4) ______________ ______________ (not regard) as being valuable. Clothes (5) ______________ (often order) online. Then a jumper or a jacket (6) ______________ (wear) just once, maybe at a party, then the goods (7) ______________ (send back) to the dealer. Fortunately, more and more people (8) ______________ (worry) by the effects of fast fashion. Clothes (9) ______________ (buy) less often by these people.

13 79/9 ## 4 You will hear an interview between a student Marcus and Alicia Lopez, the owner of an environmentally-friendly clothes shop.

Listen and take notes. You do not have to write complete sentences, but one word is not enough.

1. Who can wear Alicia's clothes?

   ____

2. Where are the new clothes made?

   ____

   ____

3. What are Alicia's principles? (3 details)

   ____

   ____

4. Why are the clothes often quite expensive? (3 details)

   ____

5. What types of clothing are recycled? (3 details)

   ____

6. Who are Alicia's typical customers?

   ____

7. How do women find out about her store?

   ____

8. What does Marcus want to do after the interview?

   ____

79/10 5 (WRITING) Write an e-mail of enquiry.

You have found out from a friend about an environmental group called Better Tomorrow that organises clothes swaps. You would like to take part in one of their events and swap some of your clothes.
Write them an e-mail of enquiry.

Write about 200 words. Include the following:
- ask when and where the next event is
- ask how you can sign to take part
- find out how the event works
- write your opinion about events like this
- one additional aspect

82/6 ⇗ **1** (READING) Read the story.

21st Century Pirates

A "I'm so jealous," said Sabrina, Anthony's sister. "You're going to spend two weeks on a yacht in the Caribbean, and I'm going to spend three weeks camping in a caravan. It's not fair!"
Anthony laughed and checked his passport and his ticket again. He couldn't believe it! His friend Hadrian had invited him to spend two weeks on his family's yacht. He was meeting Hadrian and his dad at the airport in Barbados and was a little nervous. He wanted to make a good impression. He didn't know Hadrian that well, but he really liked him and was looking forward to getting to know him better.
"Make sure you call us," said Anthony's mum. "Hadrian's father told us there is Wi-Fi on the yacht, and he has just bought a satellite phone." "Yes, Mum, don't worry," said Anthony.

B Hadrian and his father picked Anthony up from the airport and then they took a taxi to the yacht. Anthony's excitement grew as he saw the yacht in the sun. He couldn't believe this would be his home with Hadrian for the next two weeks! Anthony really enjoyed his first week on the yacht. They drove to different islands in the Caribbean, and Anthony worked side by side with Hadrian on the boat and learned something new every day. After a few days Anthony felt like a completely different person.

C Then one evening, while Anthony was washing the plates from dinner, he heard shouts above him and the sound of heavy boots. 'That's strange,' he thought because one of the first things Hadrian's dad had told him was to take his shoes off when he was on the yacht. Then he heard Hadrian's dad shout, "Please don't hurt us! Look, I have a lot of money. Come with me and you can have it!" Anthony's heart began to beat faster. Were there pirates on the yacht? Would they hurt Hadrian? What would they do if they saw him? He quickly hid behind the kitchen door.

D Hadrian and his father came down with three men, who were carrying long knives. They had masks over their faces, so he could only see their eyes. "Is it just the two of you on the yacht?" shouted one of the pirates. "Yes, just my son and I," answered Hadrian's father. Hadrian looked around the kitchen, looking for Anthony. "Don't try to escape. We've broken your radio, so you can't call for help. Just show us where the money is."

E Anthony felt sick. What could he do? Then he remembered – the Wi-Fi! He took out his phone – no signal! Of course, they were too far out in the ocean. The only other option was the satellite phone. But where was it? Anthony looked around the kitchen. It wasn't there. The pirates had taken Hadrian and his father into the bedroom where the money was. He couldn't go and look in there. He had to try to sneak up the steps and find the phone. He slowly opened the kitchen door and looked along the short corridor. The bedroom door wasn't closed, and he could see Hadrian sitting on the bed. He ran up the steps to look for the phone. He hoped the pirates wouldn't hurt Hadrian and his father. And there it was! The satellite phone was on the table where they had had dinner. Of course, he had used it to call his mum. He grabbed the phone, but who could he call? He didn't know the number for the police. The only number in the phone was his mum's. So he called it ...

F Later that day, Anthony called his mum again. "Yes, Mum, we are all fine, thanks to you! After I called you, three boats full of police came and saved us." "Oh, Anthony! I'm so glad you're all OK! But you were all really lucky!" said his mum. 'Yes,' thought Anthony. 'I'm lucky in more ways than one.'

82/6 ↗ **2 Which of the headings (0–7) matches the paragraphs of the text (A–F) best?**

Write the correct numbers in the boxes. Use each number only once. Be careful: You do not need two of the headings.

Part A	0	The criminals make their demands
Part B	1	Uninvited guests show up
Part C	2	A great boat party
Part D	3	Getting ready to go
Part E	4	Anthony's sister can't wait
Part F	5	Anthony comes to the rescue
	6	The journey begins
	7	All's well that ends well

A	B	C	D	E	F
			0		

82/6 ↗ **3 Are the sentences true (T) or false (F)? Choose 'not in the text' (N) if there is not enough information to answer. Tick (✓) the correct answer.**

	T	F	N
1. Anthony and his sister are really looking forward to their stay on the yacht.	☐	☐	☐
2. Hadrian has been Anthony's friend for the last five years.	☐	☐	☐
3. Anthony enjoyed learning about life on a boat.	☐	☐	☐
4. Anthony learned a lot on the yacht.	☐	☐	☐
5. Anthony heard the pirates before he saw them.	☐	☐	☐
6. Anthony didn't see what weapons the pirates had.	☐	☐	☐
7. The satellite phone was in the kitchen.	☐	☐	☐
8. The pirates never wanted to hurt Hadrian and his father.	☐	☐	☐
9. Anthony had called his mum earlier that evening.	☐	☐	☐
10. Anthony, his mum and the police all saved the day.	☐	☐	☐

● **4 (WRITING) Write another part of the story.**

82/6 ↗

What do you think happened when the police arrived? Write this part of the story with your own ideas.

Lösungen online
84k4a4

___/6P

1 I can understand information about different aspects of globalisation.

→p. 58/1

The paragraphs of the text are mixed up. Put the parts (A–F) into the right order (1–6).

The history of globalisation

☐ A Not long after this a series of scientific discoveries resulted in the Industrial Revolution. Using the new machinery and raw materials from the colonies, European countries introduced mass-produced goods for the home market and the colonies.

☐ B What do you think of when you hear the word 'globalisation'? Probably things like the 'World Wide Web', 'multinational companies' or 'container ships from China'.

☐ C In conclusion, it must be said that globalisation can have its advantages or disadvantages, depending on who you are and where you live. It would be good if those who benefit from it could take more responsibility for those on the losing side.

☐ D Today those colonies have become independent countries and our experience of globalisation is different. Global trade is now regulated by international agreements; transport is cheaper and quicker and goods from abroad cost less. But jobs are also exported to where wages are lower.

☐ E A few centuries later new parts of the globe were discovered and explored, in the Americas, for example. Traders travelled by land and sea in search of goods and European nations established and exploited colonies.

☐ F But in fact globalisation is really old. It goes back to the Ancient Greeks and Romans, who traded with other countries all over the world. Of course, their world was much smaller than the one we know today.

___/14P

2 I can talk about trade in Asia.

→p. 58/2

Complete the following text. Use the correct form of the words in brackets and find words of your own to replace the question marks.

In the past few years, more and more goods (1) ______________________ (import) from Asia, most of (2) ______________ (???) from China. But Western companies not only (3) ___________ (buy) products in containers, but (4) _______________ (???) services, especially from IT companies. Today India is the (5) ________________ (???) important country in the world for global technology. Experts predict that the Indian economy (6) ____________________ (grow) by 8 % in the next two years. When India (7) __________________ (start) to export IT services in the 1970s, there were several problems (8) ______________________ (???) needed to be solved. Employees had to speak English (9) _______________ (good). For some years there were (10) ___________________ (serious) doubts about security in India, but European and American firms (11) ____________________________ (attract) by the low costs. Indian employees earned less (12) _______________ (???) Western workers and they didn't mind (13) ___________________ (work) long hours. But that may change, now the standard of living (14) ___________________ (rise) for qualified Indians.

___/5P 3 I can understand a website about a Fairtrade project.

→ p. 58/3

Read the text in your book on page 74 again. Then answer the questions. Write short answers.

1. What promise has the school made to the cooperative? ______
2. What does the school get in return? ______
3. What did Ivy notice one day in the supermarket? ______
4. Why do the farmers have to use pesticides? ______
5. What has changed in the school canteen? ______

___/5P 4 I can write a formal e-mail.

→ p. 59/4

You want to have a birthday party in August with about 50 guests with food and music at a place called the Party Centre. Write an e-mail of enquiry to them. Write a suitable beginning and ending and ask about the following things: available dates, vegan and vegetarian menus, available products from local farmers and supermarkets, and DJs.

______

______

______

______

______

______

______

___/6P 5 I can understand a story about modern transport.

→ p. 59/5
14

Listen to a reporter and a police officer talking about the events (page 54 of the workbook) and fill in the missing information.

Name of yacht ______

When? ______

Where? ______

Info about pirates? ______

Info about owner? ______

Press conference? ______

Lösungen online 84k4a4

○ 1 I can understand information about different aspects of globalisation.

Match the sentence parts.

1. Globalisation gives many people the chance …	a new life elsewhere.
2. Today it is possible for people or companies to …	their jobs are outsourced.
3. We can communicate with the whole world with the help…	considering the local people.
4. Refugees who have to flee often manage to start …	important education is.
5. More and more governments are beginning to realise how …	of digital technology.
6. Multinational firms exploit natural resources without …	losing their jobs.
7. When people protest about the damage, they risk …	buy or sell goods anywhere.
8. Some workers become redundant when …	to travel around the world.

○ 2 I can talk about trade in Asia.

Put the sentences in the dialogue in the right order.

1. "Li Yoo what? Is it far from here?" ☐
2. "No, I have enough shoes. I'd like to buy something that reminds me of my trip to Asia" ☐
3. "Great, I'll get my bag. Let's go!" ☐
4. "Tomorrow's my last day in Hong Kong. I'd like to go to a market." ☐
5. "No, just two blocks away. We can walk there." ☐
6. "The best place for Chinese souvenirs is Li Yuen Street." ☐
7. "Good idea. Do you want to buy something? Sneakers?" ☐

○ 3 I can understand a blog about a Fairtrade project.

Read the text on page 50 of your workbook again. Tick the statements that are true.

1. Miguel got money from Fairtrade to buy his house. ☐
2. After he had left school, Miguel started working in a Fairtrade office. ☐
3. The people at Fairtrade tell the farmers how they should spend the money they earn. ☐
4. Luis doesn't have time to play football or basketball. ☐
5. Many young people leave school before they reach the final class. ☐
6. Miguel hopes his son will go to university. ☐

○ 4 I can write a formal e-mail.

You ordered a coat, but the company sent you the wrong size, large instead of medium. Write an e-mail to the company asking them if they can send you the correct size by the end of the week. You ordered coat 35252 and your customer number is ZR56M45.

○ 5 I can understand a story about modern transport.

Read the text on page 54 in your workbook again. Then decide: Who could say or think this? Write the correct name next to each statement.

What an adventure! Who knew sailing could be so great? I wish I had a boat.

Those three guys were really lucky! Good thing we could get there in time.

My camping trip was great after all. And it wasn't as dangerous as my brother's trip!

I felt really helpless when I saw the pirates. I'm just glad the boys weren't hurt.

We would not have hurt anyone, but we are still in really big trouble.

I hope Anthony wants to sail with us again. It was great having a friend on the boat.

I felt really helpless and I hope Anthony doesn't get asked to go on Hadrian's boat again. I think it's too dangerous. I'm glad the boys weren't hurt.

Here you can improve your skills by doing a speaking exercise.

Partner A

Partner B

87/4

1 Talk about what you like to do on holiday.

Talk about your favourite holidays in the past or about a holiday you are going on soon.
You can also describe your dream holiday.

Make sure to be polite and friendly when talking to your partner. It is important to show your partner that you are interested in what he or she is saying. Be a good listener and ask questions now and again. Plus, try to answer your partner's questions as completely as possible. And don't forget to maintain eye contact with your partner during your conversation.

87/4

2 Take turns to describe your pictures.

a) You each choose two photos on page 60. You have one minute each to describe your photos to your partner. Listen carefully to what your partner says.

b) Now give your partner some feedback. What did he or she do well? What could have been better? Would you have described the photos differently? Remember: There are lots of different possible answers here.

● c) Do you think these photos were well chosen for this exercise? Give reasons for your answer.

Here are some tips on how to describe your photo:

Start with general information about the photos. Who can you see? What is happening? What is the atmosphere in the photos.

Then start talking about the details in the photos. Where do you think the photos were taken? Are the people in the photos friends or family members?
What do the people look like?
Are they young or old?
Do they look happy or sad?
When were the photos taken?
And who do you think might have taken the photos?
Do you think there is a story behind the photos?
For example, think of the yacht story on page 54.

87/4

3 Which picture do you prefer?

Which holiday would you prefer? Why?
What does your partner think?
Give reasons for your answer.

It can be helpful to pretend that you either really love something or that you don't like it. Or to be of the opposite opinion of your partner. That way, you will definitely have something to say.

Lösungen online
84k4a4

The future of transport

88/2

1 (MEDIATION) Verwende die Information über den *space elevator* und bearbeite die Aufgaben (1–5) stichpunktartig auf Deutsch.

Es ist keine wörtliche Übersetzung nötig, die Aspekte müssen inhaltlich jedoch vollständig erfasst sein. Einzelwörter genügen nicht als Antwort.

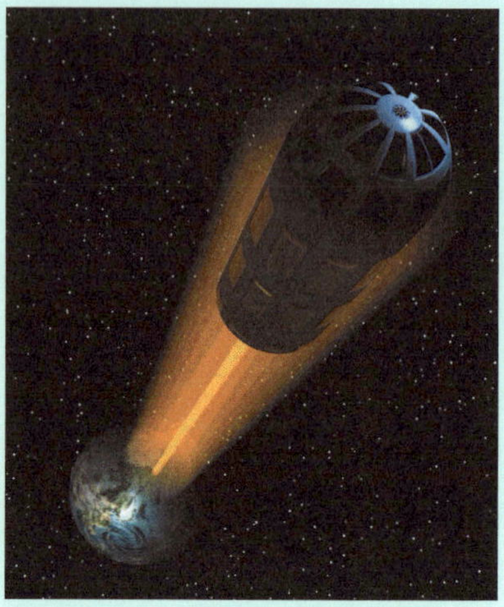

Space travel is booming. But so far the only way of getting people or things up into space has been by rocket. According to current estimates it costs about $22,000 to put a load of just one kilogram into space – and $1.3 million for one person!

For some years now scientists have been researching an alternative to rockets: a space elevator which would transport virtually anything from the earth to a space station. The cost of sending goods into space would be reduced to $200 per kilo. The system itself would be extremely expensive to install, but the investment would be repaid after some time.

How does the space elevator work? The elevator itself ('the climber') goes up and down between the earth and a space station along a long, thin cable or rope ('the tether'). The cable is fixed to a base on the earth ('the anchor'). On the space station at the other end there is a weight which holds the cable in place.

A rocket needs a constant supply of energy to reach its goal, whereas the space elevator makes use of the earth's rotation once it has gone into orbit. It all sounds like a good idea, but there are still several problems. So far no one has been able to find a suitable material for the cable. And where would the power for the elevator come from? From atomic energy or a powerful laser? Although it would be sustainable, the space elevator would be the most expensive project ever undertaken. Would it be worth it? The researchers say yes.

1. Warum wird nach Alternativen zu Raketen gesucht?

____

2. Warum wäre der Space Elevator auf lange Sicht günstiger?

____

3. Erkläre, wie der Space Elevator funktioniert.

____

____

____

4. Welche zusätzliche, natürliche Energiequelle nutzt der Space Elevator?

____

5. Welche Probleme ergeben sich aktuell bei der Planung des Space Elevator? (2 Details)

____

____

89/5

2 Complete the following text.

Use the correct form of the words in brackets and find words of your own to replace the question marks.

Hannah is a keen science fiction fan (1) ______________ (???) collection of books, games and DVDs is really (2) __________ (huge). The (3) ______________________ (inspiring) sci-fi movie she has ever seen is *Ad Astra*. She made her boyfriend (4) ____________ (watch) it with her five times! A few months (5) __________ (???) she decided to take (6) __________ (???) in a competition for 'the (7) __________ (good) science fiction short story (8) _________ (???) a teenage writer'. Hannah liked the idea of (9) ______________ (write) about a space elevator (10) ___________________ (???) could travel (11) ________________ (???) the earth and another planet without (12) _____________ (use) a cable. The (13) ____________________ (possible) of solar power were very (14) ___________________ (interest), she thought. "If my heroes can capture the sun's energy before (15) ___________ (???) enters our atmosphere, the solar power (16) ______________ (be) strong enough to send my elevator to Mars – or even (17) _______________ (far)! There are so many new discoveries (18) ________ (???) dream about! I'm really looking forward to (19) _______________ (write) my story!"

89/5

3 Complete the second sentence so that it has a similar meaning to the first sentence, using the KEY WORD given in brackets.

Do not change the KEY WORD given. You must use between two and five words including the KEY WORD.

1. Even people who look down on science fiction say they read it sometimes. (ADMIT)

   Even people who look down on science fiction ________________________________ it sometimes.
2. Space travel is probably the topic which interests the largest number of science fiction fans. (POPULAR)

   Space travel is probably the _____________________________ among science fiction fans.
3. In many stories the most frightening part is an unexpected meeting with aliens in outer space. (NOTHING)

   In many stories ____
   an unexpected meeting with aliens in outer space.
4. Famous authors have written stories about the arrival of aliens on earth. (BY)

   Stories about the arrival of aliens on earth ______________________________ famous authors.
5. Since writers don't know much about aliens, they have to invent all the details. (NOT)

   ____ aliens, writers have to invent all the details.
6. Travelling to another planet is exciting in spite of the feeling of danger. (ALTHOUGH)

   Travelling to another planet is exciting ____________________________ feeling of danger.
7. Missions sometimes fail because explorers are over-ambitious. (IF)

   Maybe missions wouldn't fail ______________________________ over-ambitious.
8. Provided that nothing goes wrong, the heroes usually return safely to earth. (LONG)

   ____________________ nothing goes wrong, the heroes usually return safely to earth.

Kia ora, New Zealand!

91/3 **1 Complete the sentences about a famous New Zealander. Use the correct form of the verbs. Sometimes you need more than one word.**

approximately | adrenaline junkie | enthusiast | indigenous | literally | rugged
to get stranded | to be made up of | to head to | earthquake | Maori | subtropical

One of the most famous New Zealanders is Sir Edmund Hillary. In 1919 he was born in Auckland, which is near a (1) ____________ region, but didn't stay in that warm climate. It wasn't long before he left his warm home and (2) ____________ the mountains. He was a real climbing (3) ____________ and even dropped out of college after two years. Climbing mountains (4) ____________ became his job. His first major climb was Mount Ollivier (1,933 m) in 1939. You could call him an early 20th century (5) ____________. The mountains he climbed kept getting higher and higher. In 1953 Hillary and his (6) ____________ guide from Nepal, Tenzing Norgay, were the first people to climb to the (7) ____________ top of the highest mountain (8,448 m) in the world: Mount Everest in the Himalayas. The Himalaya mountain range (8) ____________ (9) ____________ 50 mountains. Twenty-nine years before Hillary and Norgay, two British climbers were very close to the top, but they (10) ____________ on the mountain and probably never made it to the top. They both died. Hillary practised for Mount Everest on New Zealand's highest mountain, Mount Cook (3,724 m) – it's called Aoraki in the (11) ____________ language. In 1991 the mountain was 3,754 metres high, but in December rock and ice fell off the top, caused an (12) ____________ and the mountain lost 30 metres.

• **2 Make a fact sheet about New Zealand.**

91/3

Find more information about New Zealand online and create a fact sheet with the most important facts, for example population, currency, head of state, languages, holidays, food, costumes etc.

92/2 **1** **Use the word given in capitals at the end of some of the lines to form a word of the same word family that fits in the space in the same line.**

INTERNET

After living in New Zealand for five years, I (1) ______________ that there are stereotypes within the country too. For example, people from Auckland on the North Island are (2) ______________ because they have very busy lifestyles and think Auckland is all of New Zealand. They see themselves as (3) ______________ and are very materialistic. In the capital, Wellington, things are a little more (4) ______________ because more young, green hipsters live there. But (5) ______________, I have to (6) ______________ that they have the most restaurants and cafés, and they're the best! Most people there work for the government and the stereotype is that they're not very (7) ______________. In fact, they're called lazy. It is said that the people on the South Island are not very open towards new ideas. However, tourists think it is a really (8) ______________ place because it has the most outdoor tourist attractions. As a tourist you shouldn't (9) ______________ that there's nothing to see in the rest of New Zealand, though. It's interesting to watch the sheep and the farmers too! But go there and find out for yourself, and then you will see why you shouldn't believe in stereotypes!

OBSERVATION
CRITICISM
CONSUMPTION
CHAOS
HONEST
ADMISSION
DISCIPLINE
MAGICIAN
ASSUMPTION

93/6 **2** **Complete the following text. Use the correct forms of the words in brackets and find words of your own to replace the question marks.**

I was looking for (1) __________ (???) lot of outdoor activities on my holiday and discovered that Kaikoura on (2) __________ (???) east coast of New Zealand is a perfect place to visit – or to stay for a whole year! If you (3) ______________ (travel) in summer, you (4) ______________ (find) something new to do every day – fishing, diving and kayaking! But winter is (5) __________ (???) better time to see whales and baby seals. I (6) ______________________ (come) only in summer if I hadn't read about the snow-covered mountains from June to August. Visiting in autumn is (7) __________ (???) best time to see lots of dolphins. The spring months of October and November are some of the (8) ______________ (windy) months and that's when it's the (9) ______________ (???) crowded in Kaikoura – not many tourists at all. If Kaikoura (10) ______________ (have) a fifth season, I (11) ______________ (visit) then too!

94/7 3 Make if-clauses to complete these sentences.

1. If I found an interesting book about New Zealand, I would read it. ________ (read it)
2. If I went to New Zealand, ______________________________ (learn more about the country)
3. ______________________________ I would improve my English. (talk to people there)
4. If I could do any job in New Zealand, ______________________________ (work on a farm)
5. If I was rich, ______________________________ (help the poor)
6. ______________________________ if I had enough time. (travel around the country)
7. ______________________________ if I spent time in New Zealand. (try different foods)

94/8 4 Complete the if-clauses with the correct form.

1. If I try harder at school, I'll get ________ (get) better grades.
2. If I ________________ (want) to learn a new language, I would travel to another country.
3. If I get my pocket money on Friday, ________________ (go) shopping at the weekend.
4. If I ________________ (not understand) the homework, I would have called you.
5. I would watch that film about New Zealand if they ________________ (show) it at the local cinema.
6. I ________________ (not eat) meat if I went to that restaurant.
7. What would you have done if you ________________ (not find) your phone?
8. Where would you go if you ________________ (have) a lot of money?

94/8 5 Write the if-clauses with your own ideas.

1. If I work hard at school, ______________________________
2. If I travelled to ______________________________
3. If I won a lot of money, ______________________________
4. My family would be happy ______________________________
5. At the weekend I'll ______________________________
6. If I had a car, ______________________________

95/9 6 (MEDIATION) **Verwende die Informationen über Landkarten und bearbeite die Aufgaben (1–4) stichpunktartig auf Deutsch.**

Es ist keine wörtliche Übersetzung nötig, die Aspekte müssen inhaltlich jedoch vollständig erfasst sein. Einzelwörter genügen nicht als Antwort.

Where is New Zealand?

People often leave New Zealand off world maps; it's a country the size of the United Kingdom with a population of five million people. For example, it is not on a map at the Pyongyang International Airport in North Korea, or on the Globe Fountain at Universal Studios in Hollywood. Sometimes even geography books forget to include New Zealand on their maps. But the real surprise is a world map on one of the official government websites of New Zealand. You guessed it – no New Zealand! One can only speculate about why New Zealand is so often forgotten. Most likely the problem is that New Zealand is so far down on the right side of every map that it is easy to just cut it off by mistake.

But quite a few people did notice that New Zealand is often left off maps, and they were so unhappy about it that they started a campaign to try and make map makers aware of their mistake. There is now a website where you can post pictures of these wrong maps. Plus, check out the funny video starring famous New Zealand actor Rhys Darby and New Zealand's Prime Minister Jacinda Ardern; it shows just how widespread the problem really is. The hope is that companies and organisations will now become aware of the problem. Schools in New Zealand have also come up with a creative way to make students take more notice of their own country. Teachers have hung up new world maps on their classroom walls, and on these maps New Zealand is easy to find because it is in the centre!

Rhys Darby

So the next time you see a world map, look at it carefully. Has New Zealand been left off? If the answer is yes, then tell people about it. After all, nobody likes to be forgotten.

1. Welches Problem wird hier geschildert? Nenne dafür zwei Beispiele.

2. Warum wird das Land oft vergessen?

3. Wie versucht man, auf das Problem aufmerksam zu machen? (3 Aspekte)

4. Wie kann jeder helfen?

97/6

1 Read the text about the history of wind energy.

Wind power is not a new invention. In fact, it has been used by humans for as long as they have sailed with boats. Some of those first boats were sailed on the Nile in Egypt as early as 5000 B.C. In the 8th century, countries like Iran, Afghanistan and Pakistan used wind energy to power machines that ground grain or pumped water. Wind energy is generally easier to use than water energy because it is more available and independent of a location next to a fast-flowing river. Places in different parts of the world – China and Sicily – both used wind power around 1000 A.D. to pump seawater onto land and make salt from it. About one-third of the Netherlands is below sea level and that's why the Dutch used windmills in the early 16th century to drain lakes. They could then use the dry land for houses and agriculture. In 1887 the first windmill to generate electricity was built in Scotland. European immigrants to North America took windmill technology with them. Just like thousands of years ago, the colonists used wind energy to grind grain, pump water and even cut wood. Back in Europe, Poul la Cour, a Danish scientist and inventor, discovered in 1903 that if windmills have fewer blades and spin faster, they are more efficient. Throughout the 20th century and into the 21st, the production and use of wind energy has grown around the world. In 1991 Denmark built the world's first offshore wind farm and wind energy now covers 30 % of the country's electricity needs. The US had 581 wind farms in 2010, which produce enough electricity for ten million homes. The small country of New Zealand has 17 wind farms that produce 5 % of the country's electricity. That's enough for 300,000 homes. Most of the wind farms are located in the lower part of the North Island, where strong winds blow all year long. Some people are against them, though, because of the noise, appearance and environmental concerns. Wind farms are definitely a lot different from silent sails on the Nile.

97/6

2 Are the sentences 'True' (T) or 'False' (F)? Choose Not in the text (N) if there is not enough information to answer. Tick (✓) the correct answer.

	T	F	N
1. People used wind power to sail boats more than 7,000 years ago.	☐	☐	☐
2. A Greek engineer made the first wind-powered machine in the 1st century.	☐	☐	☐
3. Iranians used wind energy to clean water.	☐	☐	☐
4. The Dutch used windmills to get more land for farming.	☐	☐	☐
5. In 1887 England produced electricity using a windmill for the first time.	☐	☐	☐
6. La Cour increased the efficiency of windmills by reducing the number of blades.	☐	☐	☐
7. Offshore wind farms are located in oceans and seas.	☐	☐	☐
8. There are only wind farms on the North Island of New Zealand.	☐	☐	☐

99/4 **1** **Complete the text with the right words from the text on page 98 in your book.**

Tourism is one of the most important industries in New Zealand, and adventure tourism, which offers (1) _ _ _ _ - _ _ _ - _ _ - _ _ _ _ _ _ _ _ _ (l.1) experiences, has been growing every year. However, what a lot of tourists don't know is that the owners of the companies sometimes don't have to sign on the (2) _ _ _ _ _ _ _ _ _ _ _ (l.16) like their customers do. There are many (3) _ _ _ _ _ _ (l.23) about whether there are enough laws to protect the thrill-seekers. For example, for canoeing or (4) _ _ _ _ _ _ _ (l.9) trips, we think the companies should be required to have rescue ropes with them. Then a woman wouldn't have died when she fell off her raft and got stuck under some (5) _ _ _ _ _ _ _ _ (l.20). There must also be (6) _ _ _ _ _ _ _ _ _ _ _ _ _ (l.22) before the adventure begins. Then a man, whose (7) _ _ _ _ _ _ _ (l.22) was never attached to the (8) _ _ _ _ _ _ _ _ _ _ _ _ (l.14), wouldn't have died while (9) _ _ _ _ _ _ _ _ _ _ _ _ _ _ _ (l.12). Of course, customers can (10) _ _ _ (l.17) a company after an accident, but that doesn't bring the person back or heal their injuries. Before people jump (11) _ _ _ _ _ _ _ _ _ (l.25) off a cliff, they should know that the laws to protect them are in place. The New Zealand government must ensure that tourists needn't be (12) _ _ _ _ _ _ _ _ _ (l.18) about their safety when they are looking for fun and adventure. It's time for more control and laws.

99/4 **2** **(SPEAKING) Describe the cartoons.**

Work with a partner. Choose one cartoon each and describe it to your partner. Do you understand the joke? Do you think it is funny? Why/why not? These words can help you:

flightless | reindeer | look | ahead

1

"WELL I DON'T KNOW HOW *THEY* FLY WHEN I CAN'T!"

2

100/5 **3 Here are the notes Kevin took after talking on the phone with a rafting company. Write what he reported to his friend about the phone call with Kendra.**

- Rotorua region offers great rafting
- Kaituna River is located in a deep canyon
- is home to highest waterfall used by rafting companies
- will find rafting experience for every age group
- have never had an accident on their tours
- her company has been certified by the New Zealand government
- tours are filling up quickly, should book soon
- do we need hotel too? they can make recommendations

1. Kendra told me ____________________
2. She said ____________________
3. She mentioned ____________________
4. Kendra explained ____________________
5. She said ____________________
6. She explained ____________________
7. She said ____________________
8. She asked ____________________

100/6 **4 After your adventure with the Rotorua Rafting Company, you write a blog to go with your pictures. Follow the steps below.**

1. Take notes about each picture.
2. Collect adjectives and verbs to use.
3. Use at least three senses to describe your experience.
4. Report what the other adventurers thought about it.

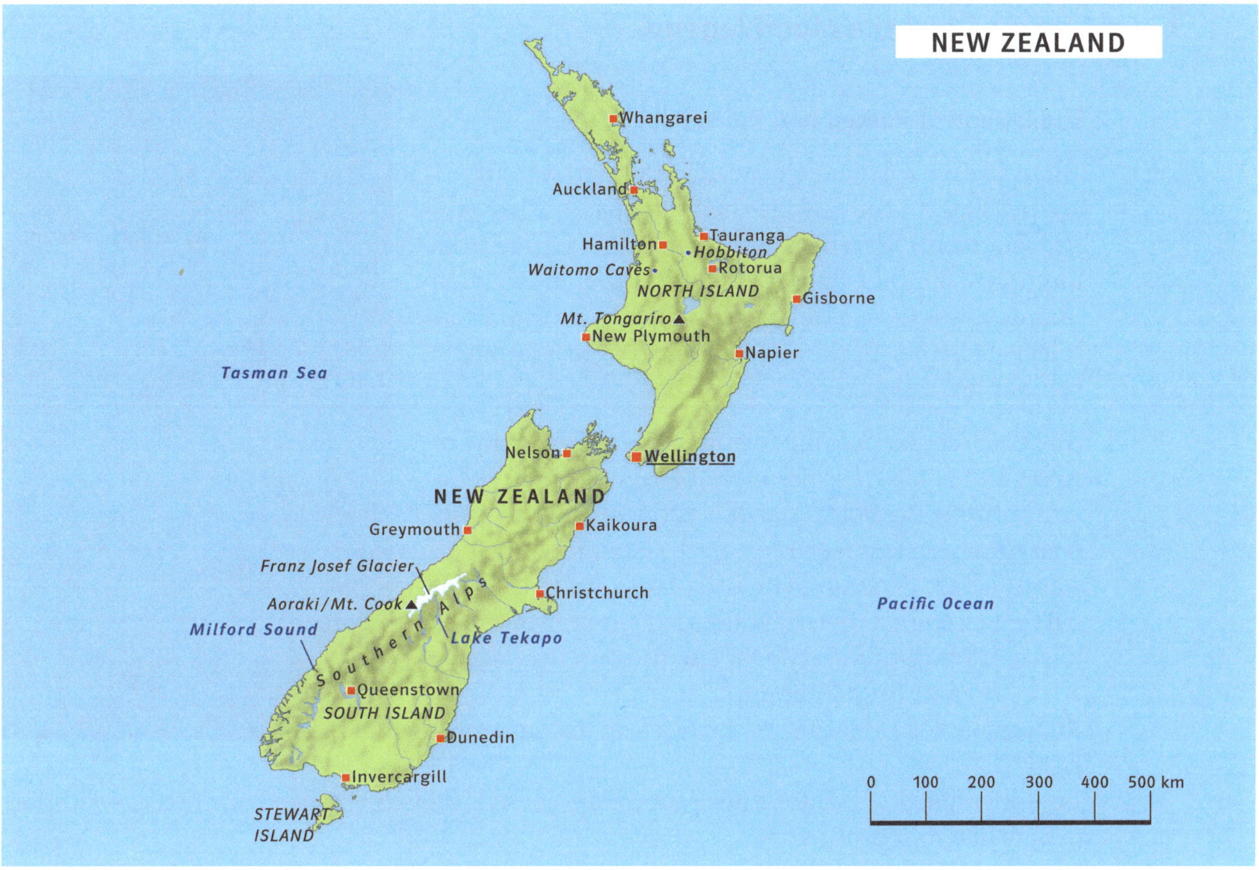

15 101/7 **5 Listen to a radio report about a bike trip in New Zealand. Then draw the route of the bike trip on the map above.**

15 101/7 **6 Listen again and choose the right answer.**

1. John and his team cycled …
   a) to make money for an organisation. ☐
   b) for fun. ☐
   c) to help a friend. ☐

2. They had a support car because they …
   a) wanted to relax in the car. ☐
   b) could not transport too much. ☐
   c) had a rescue dog. ☐

3. Two riders could not finish the trip because they …
   a) were too tired. ☐
   b) had to work. ☐
   c) were injured. ☐

4. After stopping at Lake Taupo, the riders …
   a) felt relaxed. ☐
   b) took a ferry. ☐
   c) had an accident. ☐

5. While they were riding near the ocean, they saw …
   a) some old friends. ☐
   b) Steve's sister. ☐
   c) dolphins and whales. ☐

6. They changed their plans because …
   a) they were exhausted. ☐
   b) they wanted to meet Steve's brother. ☐
   c) they had a big argument. ☐

106/9 **1** (READING) Read the Maori legend.

The legend of Paikea and Ruatapu

There was once a great chief called Uenuku who lived on the island of the gods. He had 71 sons. Seventy of the sons were chiefs because their mothers came from important families from the island. One of his sons, Ruatapu, was not a chief, though. He had no important role because his mother was not from a great family but was just a slave.

One day Uenuku decided to build a great boat made of wood for his sons. His men spent many weeks making and painting the boat. Soon it was the most beautiful boat that had ever been seen on the island. When it was finished, Uenuku invited all of his sons to the boat, where he combed their hair and tied it on top of their heads in a traditional style for chiefs. Soon they were all ready apart from Ruatapu.
Ruatapu asked his father, "Are you going to comb my hair?"
Uenuku replied, "I cannot. These combs are sacred. They can be used on chiefs and important people like your brothers."
Ruatapu said, "Am I not your son?"
Uenuku said, "You are. But your mother is a slave, so I cannot use the combs on your hair."

Ruatapu was very upset and very angry. He went and sat on a bench and started to plan his revenge. His father always treated him differently than his brothers, and they did not show him any respect. Ruatapu had had enough. Even though his mother was a slave, his father was still the chief. He felt his life was very unfair. So that evening he waited until all his brothers were eating by the fire and then he went to the ocean where the boat was tied up. He climbed inside the boat, pulled a knife out of his pocket and cut a small hole in the bottom of the boat.

The next day all the brothers and Ruatapu went to take the boat out to sea for the first time. Ruatapu was careful to put his foot over the hole he had made, so that no water could come into the boat. The boat was not only very beautiful but also very fast. It was soon far out at sea. When they could no longer see the island, Ruatapu took his foot off the hole. The water rushed into the boat. His brothers cried out and tried to throw the water out of the boat, but there was too much. The boat quickly filled with water and sank. Ruatapu held on to a piece of wood as he had his revenge watching all his brothers drown. All except one. His youngest brother, Paikea, his father's favourite, did not drown and tried to swim towards the island. Ruatapu swam after Paikea, but Paikea was not afraid.
He called to Ruatapu, "I will not drown because the god of the sea will help me."
The god of the sea heard Paikea say this and sent a great whale to Paikea. Paikea climbed onto its back and rode it towards the island.

Ruatapu was angry. He said a magic spell and sent five huge waves after Paikea. But Paikea and the whale were too fast, and they were at the island before the waves. The waves bounced off the beach and went back towards Ruatapu, so he was drowned by his own magic.

The whale had brought Paikea safely to the east coast of the North Island. Paikea's family still live there today and the whale became an island off the coast.

106/9 2 **Put the events in the correct order. Write numbers in the boxes.**

- ☐ Ruatapu cut a hole in the bottom of the boat.
- ☐ Ruatapu's own waves killed him.
- ☐ Uenuku and his men built a great boat for Uenuku's sons.
- ☐ The whale saved Paikea.
- ☐ When Paikea swam towards the island, the god of the sea sent him a whale.
- ☐ Uenuku did not comb Ruatapu's hair.
- ☐ Most of the brothers drowned.

106/9 3 **Answer the questions. Write down in which lines of the text you found the answers.**

1. Why didn't Ruatapu have an important role?
2. What did Uenuku do with his sons' hair? List two things.
3. How did Uenuku treat Ruatapu differently? Give two examples.
4. Describe the boat made for the sons. Write two facts.
5. What do you learn about Paikea in this story? Write three facts.
6. How did the god of the sea help Paikea?
7. Who still lives on the North Island?

106/9 4 **(WRITING) Do you think the story is fair? Why/why not? Write your opinion. Write about 50 words.**

Lösungen online
r3iq6z

___/3P 1 I can understand information about New Zealand.

→ p. 76/1

The North Island and the South Island

New Zealand is made up of two big islands, North Island and South Island, and about 600 smaller islands. These islands did not have any contact with other continents for over 60 million years, so some plants and animals are only found there. Before people arrived, the land had been covered in forests which were full of reptiles, spiders, insects and birds which were not able to fly. There had been almost no mammals[1] on land until the first Maori settlers arrived in the 13th century.
Over the centuries the settlers hunted birds and also brought mammals to New Zealand. Many bird species that could not fly died out because the settlers cut down a lot of forests. There are, of course, still many native birds in New Zealand, such as the South Island robin seen in the photo above. However, the kiwi is probably the most famous one. This round, brown bird is very shy, only comes out at night and cannot fly. But it has still become an important symbol of New Zealand.

1 mammal = *Säugetier*

Read the text and answer the questions.

1. What was New Zealand like before human settlers arrived? (Write two facts.)

____

____

2. Why did many birds die out? ______________________________
3. Name two birds found in New Zealand. ______________________________

___/5P 2 I can give advice about responsible tourism.

→ p. 76/2

Look at the information and write a short text with travel tips for teenagers in Wellington, the capital of New Zealand. Write at least five sentences.

WELLINGTON

- Five-minute ride in 1912 Cable Car to Kelburn Lookout, great panorama for photos
- Weta Cave Workshop: making of *The Lord of the Rings* and *Hobbit* movies, models, props, costumes, and film sets, talk to designers
- Te Papa Museum of New Zealand: earthquake simulation, 11 art galleries, natural, historical and art museums
- Seal Coast Safari: 3 hours, 4-wheel-drive vehicle, see marine wildlife and fur seals
- Helicopter flight over Wellington, 9 min. to 3 hrs, $135–920, see different scenery

____

___/5P 3 I can understand information about renewable energy.

→p. 77/3

Look at the infographics on page 96 of your book again. Answer the questions.

1. Why is the use of hydroelectric power limited? ______
2. What is the big advantage of geothermal power? ______
3. Name two steps individuals can take to reduce greenhouse gas emissions. ______
   ______
4. Why would you invest in hydroelectric power in New Zealand? ______
   ______

___/8P 4 I can write a blog about an exciting event.

→p. 77/4

Complete the following text. Use the correct forms of the words in brackets and find words of your own to replace the question marks.

Wow! Last week I went to (1) an (???) awesome music festival. It's called Earth Beat Festival Aotearoa. If I had (2) k______ (know) it was going to be so wild, I would have headed there (3) e______ (early)! At first I didn't even want to go, but then my girlfriend (4) a______ (ask) me to go with her. The bands play rock 'n' roll, house and reggae music, and it's also a zero-waste festival. (5) C______ (???) to our parents' generation, that didn't take care of (6) t______ (???) environment, we literally have to save our (7) p______ before it's too late. Music and sustainability enthusiasts from all over New Zealand get (8) t______ in Auckland for one weekend every year and it is an incredible party. You're (9) e______ (encourage) to bring your own reusable water bottles and take all your garbage home with you. The website (10) s______ (???) it was a place to explore new ideas and different ways of living.

___/6P 5 I can understand a story about different generations.

→p. 77/5

Look at the story *The Whale Rider* on pages 102–104 in your book again. Are the sentences True (T) or False (F)? Choose Not in the text (N) if there is not enough information to answer. Tick (✓) the correct answer.

	T	F	N
1. Koro Apirana's stone was white.	☐	☐	☐
2. Rawiri had always known that Kahu could swim.	☐	☐	☐
3. Nani Flowers wasn't able to dive in the deep water.	☐	☐	☐
4. Kahu and the dolphins could communicate with each other.	☐	☐	☐
5. Nani Flowers had a heart attack out in the water.	☐	☐	☐
6. Nani Flowers doesn't want Koro Apirana to know about the incident.	☐	☐	☐

Lösungen online r3iq6z

○ 1 I can understand information about New Zealand.

The North Island and the South Island

New Zealand is made up of two big islands, the North Island and the South Island. On the North Island there are three large volcanoes, and around them you can find lakes, mountains, and beaches of black sand. The east coast of the North Island has many long beaches with golden sand. Although it is smaller, the North Island has the largest cities, such as Wellington and Auckland, and 77 % of New Zealand's population live there. The larger South Island has a landscape of huge lakes, rivers, glaciers and beautiful beaches. The island also has many national and forest parks. On both islands there are big sheep farms. There are about 39 million sheep in New Zealand, but only about 4.8 million people. New Zealand is also popular with filmmakers because of its great variety of landscapes, so many famous films were made there, for example *The Lord of the Rings* or *Vertical Limit.*

Read the text and complete the sentences.

1. Around the volcanoes on the North Island there are ____________________
2. The largest cities are on ____________________ and 77 % ____________________
3. ____________________ includes lakes, rivers, glaciers and beautiful beaches.
4. New Zealand has a population of 4.8 million people, but there are ____________________ sheep.
5. Filmmakers come to New Zealand because ____________________

○ 2 I can give advice about responsible tourism.

Look at the information and complete the sentences with travel tips for Christchurch.

CHRISTCHURCH

- Port Hills: locals go here for mountain biking, hiking, picnics; used to be volcanoes
- Cardboard Cathedral: built after earthquakes in 2010 & 2011; made of cardboard tubes, wood and steel; replaced original destroyed church
- International Antarctic Centre: interactive museum, storm simulation room, blue penguins
- Quake City: museum of science, heroism, hope and loss; objects that survived earthquakes – top of cathedral, railway station clocks
- New Regent Street: pedestrian zone, best cookies and ice cream

If you want to do what New Zealanders do, (1) ____________________ ____________________ Two big tourist sites have to do with (2) ____________________ ____________________ Cardboard Cathedral is on the site of the original church that (3) ____________________ ____________________ ____________________ ____________________ to learn about the science of earthquakes and Christchurch's heroes. At the International Antarctic Centre you can experience (4) ____________________ and see (5) ____________________ After a day of sightseeing, New Regent Street is a good place to (6) ____________________

○ 3 I can understand information about renewable energy.

Look at the infographics on page 96 of your book again. Match the sentence parts. Draw lines.

1. New Zealand uses fossil fuels	if they find a way to store the energy.
2. Hydroelectric power has played a big role	if they receive money from the government.
3. The government is planning to build more wind farms	for more than 100 years.
4. Businesses will decide to decarbonise	for about 20 % of its electricity.
5. Hydroelectric power could be more profitable	because New Zealand is a windy country.

○ 4 I can write a blog about an exciting event.

Complete the following text. Use the correct forms of the words in brackets and find words of your own to replace the question marks.

If you want to experience some real Maori (1) cu________ (???), go to Whakarewarewa – The Living Maori Village. The Maori people here have (2) w________ (welcome) visitors into their homes (3) f________ (???) over 200 years. They offer guided (4) t________ (???) of the village, where you can see how they cook their meals using the geothermal pools in and around the village. They also bathe in the pools and use the (5) e________ to heat their houses in winter. Three times a day there is a cultural performance with (6) tr________ (???) singing and dancing, including the haka dance. The Maori villagers will also give you a traditional tattoo if you want. You can stay overnight in the village or at Hot Water Beach Campground. You can get to the campground by (7) f________ (???), which takes four to five hours of hiking on the Tarawera Trail, or water taxis are available but must be (8) b________ (book) ahead of time. You have to bring all (9) y____ (???) own equipment and, most importantly, all (10) t________ (???) water you will need. The water in the lake or river cannot be used for drinking or preparing your food.

○ 5 I can understand a story about different generations.

Look at the story "The legend of Paikea and Ruatapu" on page 72 in your workbook again. Are the sentences True (T) or False (F)? Choose Not in the text (N) if there is not enough information to answer. Tick (✓) the correct answer.

	T	F	N
1. It took many months for Uenuku to build the boat.	☐	☐	☐
2. The sacred combs were made by the boys' mothers.	☐	☐	☐
3. Ruatapu used fire to make a hole in the bottom of the boat.	☐	☐	☐
4. Ruatapu hid the hole with his foot.	☐	☐	☐
5. Paikea's mother had taught him how to swim because he was her favourite son.	☐	☐	☐
6. Five huge whales saved Paikea's life.	☐	☐	☐

Lösungen online r3iq6z

A unique ecosystem

111/3 **1** **Look at the text on page 111 of your book again. Find a word or expression which means the same as each of the words (1–8) below.**

The lines where you can find the words or expressions are indicated in brackets.

1. to look at → ________________ (lines 1–10)
2. to do something unexpected → ________________ (lines 1–10)
3. to change because of something → ________________ (lines 11–16)
4. to develop into a risk → ________________ (lines 17–25)
5. to found → ________________ (lines 17–25)
6. to record → ________________ (lines 17–25)
7. to discover → ________________ (lines 25–30)
8. to write something → ________________ (lines 31–41)

111/3 **2** **Look at the text on page 111 of your book again. What do the following words mean?**

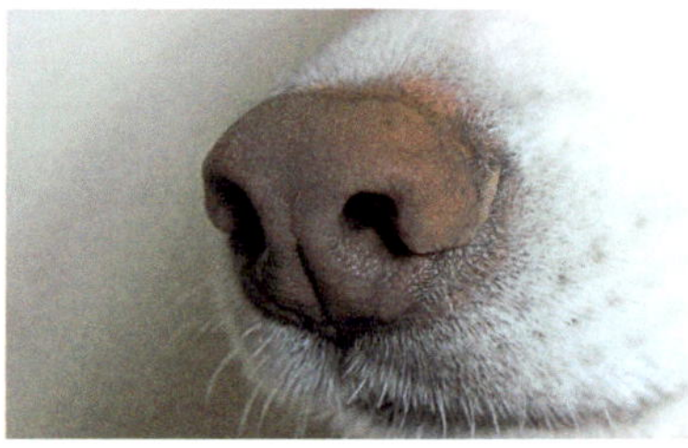

Match the expressions (A–H) as used in the text with their corresponding definitions (1–10). Write the correct numbers in the grid below. Be careful: There are two definitions that you do not need.

A luggage (line 3)
B forbidden (line 6)
C strict rules (line 11)
D diverse (line 12)
E unique (line 13)
F native (line 14)
G invasive species (line 17)
H threat (line 17)

1. being one-of-a-kind, like nothing else
2. plants or animals that don't belong to a place
3. not intending to do something
4. not allowed
5. danger or risk to people, animals or plants
6. having many different varieties
7. (big) bags to carry your things on planes, trains etc.
8. in an isolated position
9. firm regulations or list of things that you cannot do
10. indigenous or coming from the place where you are found

A	B	C	D	E	F	G	H

111/3 **3 Complete the second sentence so that it has a similar meaning to the first sentence, using the KEY WORD given in brackets.**

Do not change the KEY WORD given. You must use between two and five words including the KEY WORD.

Weta in a field

1. The famous New Zealand kiwi bird must be protected from extinction. (NECESSARY)
   ______________ to protect the famous New Zealand kiwi bird from extinction.
2. The life span of a New Zealand sea lion is about 25 years. (LONG)
   A New Zealand sea lion can ______________ ______________ 25 years.
3. There are only about 60 Maui dolphins left in New Zealand. (MANAGED)
   Only about 60 Maui dolphins ______________ in New Zealand.
4. The reptilian tuatara is a descendant of dinosaurs which lived some 200 million years ago. (KNOWN)
   ______________ that the reptilian tuatara is a descendant of dinosaurs which lived some 200 million years ago.
5. The endangered short-tailed bat can only be found in New Zealand. (ORDER)
   ______________ an endangered short-tailed bat, you must go to New Zealand.
6. Weta are huge New Zealand insects which look scary but aren't dangerous. (MIGHT)
   Weta ______________, but these huge New Zealand insects are not dangerous.
7. New Zealand's little blue penguins are hard to spot since they are only about 25 centimetres in height and come on land only at night. (EXPECT)
   ______________ the New Zealand little blue penguins easily since they are only 25 centimetres in height and only come on land at night.
8. Many of New Zealand's animals are endangered and may one day be extinct. (SOON)
   ______________ New Zealand's endangered animals may be extinct.
9. Not only animals but also many plants in New Zealand are endangered. (WELL)
   In New Zealand plants ______________ animals are endangered.
10. There are many programmes in New Zealand which are trying to protect endangered plants and animals. (AIM)
    ______________ many programmes in New Zealand is to protect endangered plants and animals.

Speaking skills

1 Have a general conversation.

138

a) Look at the topics in the box. Which topic would you and your partner like to talk about?

green holidays	being an only child
a person you admire	the importance (or not) of fashion trends
a dangerous job	an unforgettable event (sports, music, etc.)
school life	an experience with the police
a childhood memory	vegetarians / vegetarianism
how to protect the environment	cooking: a great hobby or an annoying task?

b) You have chosen your topic. What can you say about this topic? Use the example mind map below to help you prepare for your conversation.

These useful phrases could help you with your mind map:

I have chosen this topic because …
I'd like to talk about a person / an event / a question …
I have had some experience of … because …
The topic doesn't affect me personally, but …
First, I'd like to give some examples / talk about my personal experience …
Many people say / claim / argue that …, but I'm not so sure / I disagree.

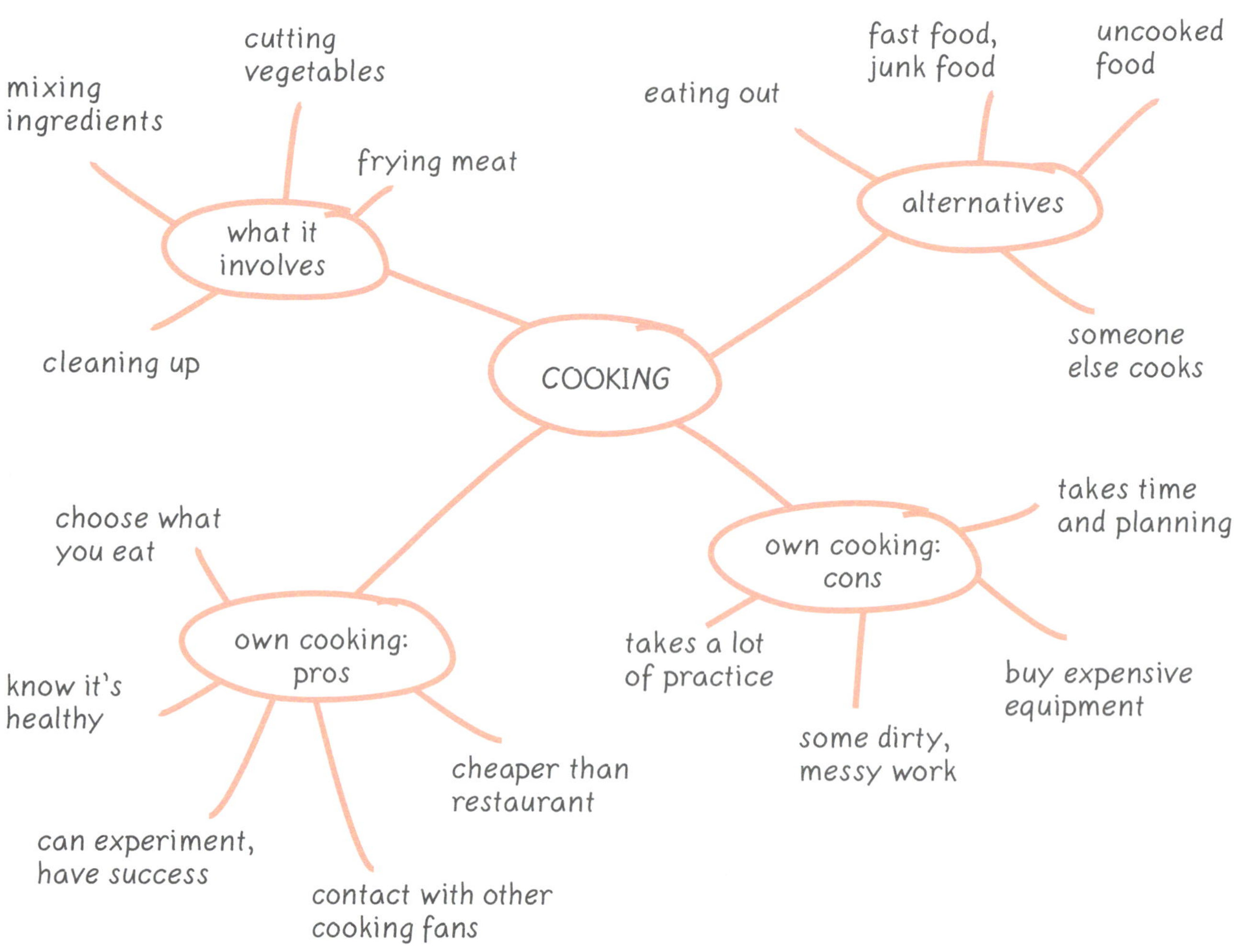

c) Here is an example of the beginning of a dialogue between two students. Read the dialogue. Then carry out a similar dialogue with your partner. Your conversation should last about three minutes.

Speaker A: Can you remember your first day at school?
Speaker B: No, not really. Only what other people have told me. What about you?
Speaker A: I can remember some things really clearly – like the new bag I had, a really cool new backpack. I really liked that bag. Do you have any memories of your first year at school?
Speaker B: Oh, yes! One day I knocked my drink over. There was red juice everywhere, so my mom had to bring me clean clothes! It was so embarrassing – not cool at all!
Speaker A: Poor you! I guess we all remember the embarrassing moments. I had quite a few. The worst was when …

→ Here are some tips for starting a conversation and keeping it going.
- You can start with a comment on the topic you have chosen. (I'm sure we'll agree / disagree on some of the points.)
- Or you can start with a question, but not one that your partner can answer with yes or no. (Why do you think people criticize …?)
- Always show a positive interest in your partner's ideas. Maintain eye contact and show a reaction like nodding agreement or smiling at a joke.
- Ask extra questions if you think your partner could give more information.
- Present a different opinion without being aggressive. This can encourage discussion. (I've heard about different experiences / opinions.)

d) How did your conversation go? Were you and your partner able to talk for three minutes? What went well? What did not go so well? What could you do better next time? Make a few notes here so you don't forget your ideas.

What went well
- concentrated on each other – conversation kept going
- asked lots of questions

Not so good
- parts of dialogue did not connect well together
- I talked about myself too much

Do better next time
- more positive feedback for partner
- don't agree all the time; give different points of view

2 Compare and contrast the two pictures.

137

a) Partner A talks about photo A separately first and then about photo B. Then compare and contrast the two photos. Pay attention to both similarities and differences. Use the same structure for your description of each photo; for example, talk about the setting, then the people, their clothes and their activities. Then your partner can follow your short talk more easily. Then comment on the atmosphere in the photo and the possible thoughts and feelings of the people. Give reasons for your interpretation.

Photo A
Happy customer

Quickly describe the photo.

The people:
- Who is in the photo?
- What do they look like?
- What are they doing / saying?
- How do they feel?
- Why do you think that?

Photo B
Unhappy customer

Quickly describe the people in the photo using the questions from photo A.

Compare the photos:
- What's the same? What's different?
- How must the waitress and waiter react differently to the situations?
- Which situation do you find more interesting?

b) Talk about how difficult or easy it is to deal with customers in general.

c) Now partner B talks about photo A separately first and then about photo B. Then compare and contrast the two photos. Pay attention to both similarities and differences. Use the same structure for your description of each photo; for example, talk about the setting, then the people, their clothes and their activities. Then your partner can follow your short talk more easily. Then comment on the atmosphere in the photo and the possible thoughts and feelings of the people. Give reasons for your interpretation.

Photo A
Working out at the gym

Quickly describe the photo.

The people:
- What do they look like?
- What are they doing/ saying?
- How do they feel?
- Why do you think that?

Photo B
Sports with friends outside.

Quickly describe the people in the photo using the questions from photo A.

Compare the photos:
- What's the same? What's different?
- What are the relationships between the people in the photos?
- Which photo can you relate to more?

d) At the end you can talk about the best places to do sports.

137

3 Talking about a photo from a certain perspective.

a) Read the dialogue between two teenagers who are discussing the topic: Can men and women always do the same jobs?

Women and men in the world of work

Why are some jobs done more by women and some more by men? Can you think of any jobs where this is true? Do you think this is good or bad? What problems can it cause if not everyone has a fair chance to do a certain job? Can you think of specific examples?

Teen 1: I'll start. Did this photo surprise you?
Teen 2: No, it didn't. Why should it? What is surprising about a woman at work?
Teen 1: You must admit it is unusual. Women don't often drive fork lifts.
Teen 2: You have a very old-fashioned view. Women today can do any job. What's wrong with that?
Teen 1: Well, you need physical strength for this kind of work.
Teen 2: Sorry, but you're wrong there. Machines do all the lifting in a modern warehouse.
Teen 1: I'm not convinced. Think of the repairs and the heavy tools. And what about bullying?
Teen 2: A woman can learn to work with tools just as well as a man. But I see your point about bullying. Men don't always accept women in their world. It often depends on their boss.
Teen 1: You're right there! Maybe things will get better when more of the bosses are women!

Here are some tips to help you talk about a photo and a situation:

Getting started
- Decide who is going to talk first.
- Start with a general statement about the photo. (They all look very unhappy. I'm glad it isn't me!)

Developing a discussion
- Talk about the issues behind the photo. (I think this is typical of … / Nobody ever tries …)
- Present contrasting opinions. (Many people would disagree with you because …)

Finishing up
- Sum up the points that you agree on. (We both agree on … / We both see eye to eye on …)
- Say which differences between you cannot be solved. (We could not compromise on … / We cannot agree on the following…)
- Think about what you have learned from your discussion. (I can see your point. Now I understand why …)

b) Now discuss a problem or a situation in one of these photos with your partner. You can use the notes under the photos. Don't forget to look at the example dialogue and tips on page 84 for help.

Conflicts between teenagers and their parents

What do teenagers and parents often argue about? What do you think the argument in this photo could be about? How do you experience arguments with your parents? What about your friends? How can conflicts between teenagers and parents be reduced? How can each side learn to better understand the other side? Is it good if people never argue?

A

Wearing a uniform

What are the advantages of wearing a uniform at work or in other places like schools? For example, does it help to explain your position at work? What are the disadvantages of wearing a uniform? Does it take away a person's individuality? Have you ever worn a uniform at work or at school? What did these experiences teach you?

B

Lawbreakers

Have you ever seen a crime? How did you feel? How would you feel if you saw someone stealing? Angry? Frightened? Would you care? Would you get involved? (Shout at criminal, call police, run away…) What about less serious crimes? (A friend leaves garbage on the beach, uses the bus without paying …)

C

An ideal holiday

How are these holidaymakers spending their time? What kind of people are they? What do you think they like about their holiday? Is this a good holiday or not? (Impact on the environment, need for emergency services, etc.) What is your opinion? Discuss your idea of an ideal holiday.

D

137

4 A monologue about a photo

adventure danger

freedom pollution

a) Look at these photos. The two words below the photos show two ways of thinking about the photos. Each partner chooses one of the photos and one of the words.

b) Each partner talks about their photo for about one minute.

Here are some ideas to help you talk about your photo:
- Explain what comes into your mind when you hear your word.
- Show your photo and describe what you can see.
- Explain the connection between your photo and the word you have chosen.
- Think about whether you have had any personal experiences to do with the subject in the photo.

c) Look at this example of how to talk about a photo.

I chose the word "work" for this photo. The word fashion makes me think of expensive clothes in shops in rich countries. The people working here are probably making clothes for stores in rich countries. They probably did not make a lot of money for their work. I have seen reports on social media about textile workers in Asia. They are not treated well by their bosses or by the shop owners in other countries. I think most of the profit goes to the owners of the factories and shops. I would like to pay more money for my clothes, but it is often difficult to find out which companies are good to their workers.

work fashion

5 Useful phrases for a discussion

a) Here are some useful phrases which you can use for a discussion. Write the phrases under the correct heading in the table below.

I suppose you're right.	No way!	Absolutely!
I see your point, but …	The way I see it, …	Neither do I.
It seems to me that …	If you ask me, …	As far as I'm concerned, …
No doubt about it.	That's not how I see it.	I'm not so sure about that.

your opinion	agreeing	disagreeing

b) With your partner discuss the following topic: Don't judge people by their appearance. Look at the photos below for ideas for your discussion. Also, use as many of the phrases from part a) as possible.

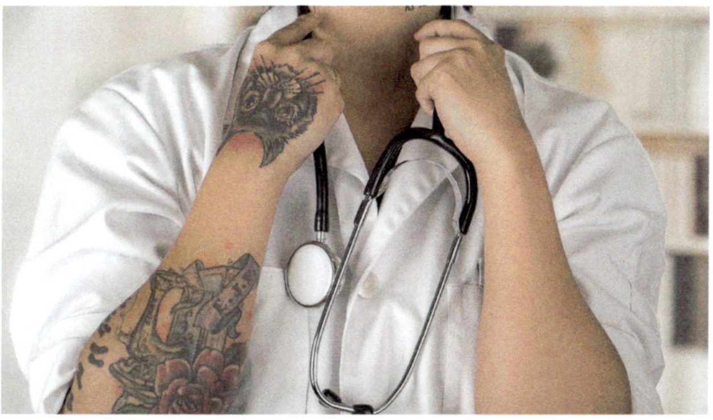

c) Give your partner feedback about the discussion. What do you think went well? What did not go very well?

Audios zum Hörverstehen

Aufnahmeleitung: Ernst Klett Verlag GmbH, Stuttgart
Produktion: John Green, TEFL Audio, London
Sprecherinnen und Sprecher: Sophie Aldred, Jenny Bryce, Joe Gaminara, James Goode, Harriet Kershaw, Toby Laurence, Kate Lock, Roger May, Rachael Miller, Gina Murray, Paul Panting, Chris Pavlo, Nigel Pilkington, Christopher Ragland, Penny Rawlins, Taryn Ryan, Matt Wycliffe

Tontechnik: Tim Woolf
Gesamtzeit: 42' 42"

Inhaltsverzeichnis der Audios zum Hörverstehen: Hörverstehenstexte aus dem Workbook

Zusätzlich enthalten: die Lesetexte des Schülerbuchs

1. Auflage 1 6 5 4 3 | 27 26 25 24

Alle Drucke dieser Auflage sind unverändert und können im Unterricht nebeneinander verwendet werden.
Die letzte Zahl bezeichnet das Jahr des Druckes.

Herausgeber: Dr. Frank Haß, Kirchberg
Autorinnen und Autoren: Jennifer Baer-Engel, Göppingen; Jo Cummins, Westgate-on-Sea; Elizabeth Daymond, Kiel
Beratung: Christine Jauch, Weitramsdorf; Nina Sklenar, Neumarkt

Entstanden in Zusammenarbeit mit dem Projektteam des Verlages.

Externe Redaktion: Birgit Piefke-Wagner, Korntal-Münchingen
Gestaltung: know idea, Freiburg; Koma Amok, Stuttgart; Marion Köster, Stuttgart
Umschlaggestaltung: know idea, Freiburg; Koma Amok, Stuttgart
Titelbilder: Avenue Images GmbH, Hamburg (Jack Hollingsworth/Blend Images); Getty Images RF, München (pjjones)
Satz: Marion Köster, Stuttgart
Reproduktion: Schwabenrepro GmbH, Stuttgart
Druck: Himmer GmbH Druckerei, Augsburg

Printed in Germany
ISBN 978-3-12-546981-5

9 783125 469815